# TELL IT LIKE IT IS

The Virgin
Young Person's
Survival Guide

## KATIE MASTERS

First published in Great Britain in 2003 by
Virgin Books Ltd
Thames Wharf Studios
Rainville Road
London W6 9HA

A catalogue record for this book is available from the British
Library.

ISBN 0 7535 0743 9

Type design by Smith & Gilmour
Typeset by Anita Ruddell
Printed and bound in Great Britain by
Mackays of Chatham plc, Chatham, Kent

# CONTENTS

# INTRODUCTION

There's a lot to deal with as you get older. Like it's not enough that your body's sprouting hair all over the place and your family's driving you mad, you're also facing decisions about everything from sex and drugs to what you should do with your future. Yikes!

You're the only person who can make those decisions about your life, but it'll be a lot easier to make them if you know what's involved. That's why this book's been written – to give you the info you need. Hope it's helpful!

# 1 YOUR BODY

Puberty is the time when your body changes from being a kid's body to being an adult's body and become sexually mature. When those changes start happening, it can make people feel really self-conscious about the way they look. The problem is that no one ever seems to think they look good enough ...

*Ariadne, 14, says: 'I'm a size 10. My thighs are too fat, my stomach's too fat, my arms are too fat, my breasts are too small and I don't like my face.'*

*Ian, 15, says: 'I wish I was bigger. I'm shorter than half the girls in my year and I've got skinny legs.'*

Heck, if you're not too thin you're too fat, if you're not too tall you're too short, if your hair's blond it should be dark ... enough already!

OK, so almost everyone has *something* about them that they wouldn't mind changing; but pretty much everyone has things about them that other people think are sexy . Usually the people who are the most attractive are the ones who are confident enough in themselves and their personalities that they don't get obsessed with the way they look.

*Lee, 18, says: 'I really fancy confident girls. I don't mean arrogant people – I mean girls who have something to say and who are willing to laugh at themselves. I can't stand it when girls think it's enough just to look pretty.'*

*Kerry, 15, says: 'You can think someone's good-looking but you only want to go out with someone if you like their personality. There's always something about a boy that seems cute if you like them as a person.'*

So maybe instead of staring in the mirror and wishing we didn't have skinny knees, acne, glasses, chunky hips or big noses, we should all start focusing on the things we like about our bodies.

*Tamsin, 16, says: 'I like my mouth. It's big and pouty and kissable!'*

*M-J, 15, says: 'Girls seem to like my bum!'*

*Amy, 17, says: 'I like my breasts. They're small but they're perfect!'*

The way you feel about your body will influence the way other people feel about your body. If you rate it, chances are other people will too. If you hate it, you'll act so self-conscious and shy, other people will figure there's got to be a reason for you behaving like that. So, the sooner you fall in love with yourself, the better!

# EATING

Some people have BIG problems with food. They seem to think eating is a bad thing and they spend their whole life going on about the fact that they're on a diet. But food isn't a bad thing – food is a fun thing. You just have to make sure that you don't eat way more than you need to and that you eat a balance of different types of food. If you scoff away at junk food the whole time, your body isn't going to be happy, but it's just as bad if you only ever eat lettuce.

So what do you need? Firstly, you need to try and make sure that you eat something from each of the following food groups every day:

→ **Carbohydrates. Carbohydrates are food like bread, rice, pasta or potatoes. They give your body energy and contain fibre that is good for your digestive system (and your bowels!).**

→ **Fruit and veg. Fruit and vegetables contain loads of vitamins and nutrients that make your body glow with health! Try and eat at least three servings of fruit or veg a day and don't always stick to your favourite – branch out, because different ones contain different vitamins.**

→ **Protein. Protein is found in food like meat, tofu, nuts, cheese and eggs. You need protein to help build and repair body tissue.**

→ **Fat. You get fats in food like butter or cheese or milk. People make a fuss about fat but everyone needs to eat a bit because it's necessary for your digestive system and to help the body produce hormones. So eat some – but don't spend all day scoffing ice cream (sorry!).**

You also need to forget about going on a diet. When people diet they often do their bodies more harm than good. That's because they're depriving themselves of essential nutrients. Plus, if your body really isn't getting all the calories it needs, it'll just hang on to all the food that comes in and won't burn it off effectively. Then when you get so hungry you have to start eating normally, your body will keep on hanging on to the food because it thinks you might be about to starve it again. It just doesn't work. If you want to lose weight, then the best thing to do is to work out a good exercise plan and make sure you're eating a balance of the necessary foods.

It's also not a good idea to skip breakfast. If you've been asleep for hours, your body needs some food to get it going again. If you wait until lunchtime then it won't be able to digest and burn off the food as effectively as it could have done if you'd eaten earlier.

The other thing to do when you eat is to listen to your body. Don't eat just because a plate of food is slapped in front of you – eat as and when you feel hungry and stop eating when you're not hungry any more.

## EATING DISORDERS

*Nicole, 18, says: 'I was really depressed when I started college. My dad had lost his job and everyone was arguing at home, I'd just split up with my boyfriend and I felt really self-conscious about myself. I thought I was fat and ugly and that's why he'd dumped me. Then I made friends with this girl – Karen – and she started telling me about her eating problems. She used to buy carrier bags full of food – always stuff like chocolates and crisps and cakes and bread and jam – eat until her stomach was really painful and then throw it all up.*

*She said she did it 'cos it gave her something to think about apart from all her other problems.*

*So I started doing it too. It was weird – it felt like a buzz to be able to eat that stuff and then get rid of it. Karen did this thing called colour layering. First she used to eat all pink things – those wafer biscuits and nougat and jam – and then she used to eat things like bread and brown biscuits and cake. Then when she threw up she'd know how much her stomach had emptied by the colour of the vomit.*

*She used to stick her middle finger down her throat and she ended up with this really rough patch of skin where her teeth kept scraping against her finger. She got bad stomach pains too 'cos she was damaging her stomach lining, and the vomit meant her teeth started to rot.*

*My breath didn't smell like hers 'cos before I made myself sick I used to drink as much water as I could. Loads and loads of it until my stomach really swelled up. Then I'd make myself sick and all the food would come out in a torrent of water and finally the water would be clear and I knew all the food was gone.*

*I stopped after about a year – me and Karen had a big falling out 'cos she was getting even weirder about what she'd do to herself – but sometimes when I'm depressed I still think about making myself sick. It just used to make me feel more in control.'*

## What is an eating disorder?

An eating disorder is an illness. It's not the same as having an allergy to a certain type of food or not liking the taste of something and it's not the same as going on a diet.

An eating disorder is about someone choosing to eat in a way that seriously damages his or her health.

## Why would anyone do that?

People develop eating disorders because controlling what they eat is a way of dealing with unhappiness. When people feel bad about themselves – or when things go wrong – they make the decision that although they can't control what's going on in the rest of their life, they can control what they eat.

Food can become something that comforts them too. When some people are unhappy or angry or stressed, they eat to block out those feelings.

Or people develop eating disorders because they think they should look a different way. What starts off as a diet can turn into an obsessive need to control the amount they weigh and the way they look.

But, although eating disorders start because people want to have a sense of control over their lives, slowly their eating disorders start to control them and they don't feel able to stop eating in a dangerous way.

## What might cause an eating disorder?
→ Feeling pressured to look a certain way.
→ Copying the eating habits of someone who doesn't eat healthily.
→ Feeling under stress.
→ Trying to cope with something that makes you unhappy.

## Who gets eating disorders?
Anyone – any age, any sex, any colour – can develop an eating disorder. Boys get them, girls get them, children get them, adults get them.

*Greg, 17, says: 'I've always been fat. I was picked last to be on sports teams and other people used to make fun of the way I looked. One time in Chemistry, the teacher made everyone pretend to be electrons but she made me pretend to be a neutron 'cos I was the biggest. It really upset me but it wasn't something I could talk to anyone about – it was too shameful. But it made me even more depressed and I started trying to diet. Mum worked and I used to get food for myself so I didn't have to worry about her noticing. At first I tried eating healthy things – pasta and fruit and vegetables – but I was losing weight really slowly so I tried just eating fruit. If I felt hungry I drank low-cal fizzy drinks to fill myself up. Then I started going swimming every morning too. It was working – my clothes were starting to become looser and Mum told me I'd slimmed down. I was getting really obsessed with it though. I wouldn't let myself eat anything except fruit and I was even trying to cut down on the amount of fruit I was eating. I think I was going a bit mad! But then one day I saw this friend of mine, Sally, who had been away at boarding school, and she just looked at me and asked me what I'd been doing to myself. She was really angry and it was starting to wind me up but then she burst into tears. She said her cousin had anorexia and the doctors had told her parents she might die. Sally said I was becoming anorexic too.*

*I didn't even know boys could be anorexic but Sally really shocked me. I can't say I changed immediately – and I still feel guilty about eating food like chocolate or crisps – but I did start eating more than just fruit. Now I try and exercise instead of watching what I eat.*

*I don't know if I had anorexia – or if I was getting that way – but I know the diet thing was starting to take over my life.'*

## ANOREXIA NERVOSA

**Anorexia nervosa** is an eating disorder where people are terrified at the thought of putting on weight. They starve themselves so their bodies become shrivelled and skinny and they don't get the vitamins and nourishment they need to stay healthy. But they can't judge how their bodies look – even when they're dangerously thin they still believe they're fat. Anorexia nervosa can end up killing people.

### How can you tell if someone is anorexic?
It's hard to tell if someone is anorexic. At first it might just seem like they're dieting – and you might not be able to tell how much weight they've lost because of the clothes they wear. These are some of the symptoms of anorexia, but every individual is different. Some people might show all the symptoms and other people might only have a few of them ...

→ Obsession with looks and with food.
→ Believing they're fat – even if they're not.
→ Not eating properly.

→ Being cold all the time.

→ Wearing baggy clothes to hide their body.

→ Having big mood swings.

→ Lacking in energy.

→ Having dry, cracked skin.

→ Dizziness.

→ Being restless.

→ Lying about what they've eaten and when.

→ Feeling depressed and emotional.

→ Losing weight.

→ Doing excessive amounts of exercise.

→ When girls become anorexic their periods can stop or become irregular.

→ Stomach pains and constipation.

## What can anorexia nervosa do to people?

→ It can make people feel really cold and give them bad circulation.

→ It can make soft hairs grow on their bodies to try and keep them warm.

→ It can make their skin dry and cracked and their hair lifeless.

→ It can damage their growth.

→ It can make girls' periods stop and boys lose their sex drive.

→ It can slow down people's reflexes.

→ It can make people's stomachs, faces and ankles swell up.

→ It can make people's bones thin and eventually make them more likely to break.

→ It can make people's muscles waste away.

→ It can make people's kidneys and hearts fail.

→ It can kill people.

## *BULIMIA NERVOSA*

**Bulimia nervosa** is an eating disorder where people eat and then make themselves sick or exercise frantically. It's hard to tell if people have this condition because their weight often stays about the same.

### How can you tell if someone has bulimia nervosa?

These are some of the symptoms of bulimia but every individual is different. Some people might show all the symptoms and other people might only have a few of them ...

→ They miss meals.
→ They lie about what they've eaten and when.
→ Their weight goes up and down.
→ They often go straight to the loo after eating (to throw up the food).
→ They take laxatives (things that help people go to the loo).
→ They have dry skin and bloodshot eyes.
→ They seem tired and depressed.
→ They have sore throats and stomach-aches.
→ Their breath starts to smell.
→ Girls have irregular periods.
→ They drink lots when they eat.
→ They have big mood swings.
→ Their faces get rounder because their glands swell up.
→ They get mouth infections.
→ They have rough patches of skin on the back of their hands.

### What can *bulimia nervosa* do to people?

→ It can make them dehydrated (their bodies don't have enough water) and tired.
→ It can make them depressed.
→ It can make their teeth rot.
→ It can damage their lungs.
→ It can damage their bowels.
→ It can damage their stomachs.
→ It can damage their kidneys.
→ It can damage their hearts.

### *BINGE EATING DISORDER*

When people binge they eat lots of food in a short time. They don't stop eating when they're full up – they keep eating until they feel uncomfortable. But, unlike people with bulimia nervosa, they don't try and get the food out of their body afterwards. Often they feel desperately miserable about their weight but they try and numb those feelings by focusing on eating more.

## How can you tell if someone is binge eating?

These are some of the symptoms of binge eating disorder, but every individual is different. Some people might show all the symptoms and other people might only have a few of them ...

→ Putting on a lot of weight.

→ Weight going up and down.

→ Having bad B.O. (sweaty body odour).

→ Eating more quickly than normal.

→ Often eating on their own.

→ Being depressed.

→ Being secretive.

→ Having bad mood swings.

→ Being ashamed of going out in public.

## What can binge eating do to people?

→ It can make them put on a lot of weight.

→ It can make them feel depressed and disgusted with themselves.

→ It can give them high blood pressure.

→ It can put them at greater risk of diseases like diabetes, coronary heart disease and gall bladder disease.

## How do people recover from eating disorders?

People with eating disorders feel they need to behave in the way they do or they won't be able to cope with their lives. It's as though they're addicted to the way they eat and, just like people who are addicted to other things, they need to decide that they want to get better and to realise that their behaviour is damaging them. If you're worried about someone's eating and you confront them about it, they may well deny they've got a problem and get angry with you.

But if you're worried about someone else's eating or if you think – or know – that you've got an eating disorder, go and talk to an adult you trust about the situation. It could be a parent or a teacher or a doctor, or you could ring a group like the Eating Disorder Association (see 'Further Help' at the end of the book) and ask for their advice.

# EXERCISE

If you're one of those people who are allergic to exercise – the type who break out in blisters if they so much as look at a pair of trainers – you really need to read this.

Without exercise your body will get:
→ **Stiff**
→ **Sore**
→ **Saggy**
→ **Stressed**

With exercise you'll feel:
→ **Strong**
→ **Supple**
→ **Sorted**
→ **Smiley**

OK. Enough Ss. But you get the idea. Exercise isn't just about keeping your body a healthy weight, it's about being able to move around without aching, it's about your skin staying in good condition and it's about the way you feel. When people exercise, their brains release all these hormones called endorphins into their bodies that make them feel happy. Doing exercise is a win-win option. That doesn't mean you have to become county cross-country champion or the captain of the swimming team. It doesn't even mean you have to be sporty. All it means is you have to find some kind of exercise you enjoy and do it at least three times a week for about fifteen to twenty minutes. That could be anything from a competitive sport like badminton, football, netball or rugby, to something individual like dancing, skating, cycling, surfing or even walking your dog around the block. It doesn't matter what you do so long as your body is active. (And no, moving your fingers and playing PlayStation does not count!)

You need to stretch before you exercise and after you finish to make sure that you don't damage any of your muscles and you need to drink a lot of water (because you'll use up your fluids more quickly than you do usually). If you do pull something or feel any aches and pains, don't do any more exercise until they've gone away. Oh, and make sure you wear proper trainers that support your feet and ankles. Hey, if you do get a blister you can always put on a plaster ...

## BOYS' BODS

*Paul, 17, says: 'The worst thing about puberty for me was that I started to smell really bad. I was sweaty the whole time – I had to put on Lynx about three times a day.'*

*Darren, 16, says: 'I started getting acne this year and I tried everything to get rid of it. I spent all my money on creams and lotions but none of them worked. In the end Mum dragged me to the doctors and I've been given this medicated stuff. The spots are starting to clear up but I still hate the way my face looks.'*

*Brian, 15, says: 'Everything seemed to happen to me really quickly. My voice broke when I was ten and I didn't have a clue what was happening – and I've been over six foot since I was thirteen. I'm not big though – I'm just skinny and long.'*

Puberty starts happening to people at different ages. Some boys reach puberty when they're as young as eight and some people's bodies are still changing when they're eighteen or nineteen.

Most boys have shown some sign of change by the time they're fourteen. They might have grown hairier or their penises might have got bigger. If your body isn't changing at all, you may have delayed puberty. This usually means you're a late developer and everything will start to happen within the next year or so, but it could mean you're ill, too underweight or have hormone problems. If you're worried, it's a good idea to go and talk to your doctor.

## So what changes happen during puberty?

***You change shape*** Your feet get bigger, your arms get longer and you start getting taller. Later on, your shoulders get broader and your muscles start to develop. The changes that happen can be really noticeable and make you worry about all sorts of things – like you're too fat, too thin, too weak or too small. If you've got concerns, go and speak to a doctor.

*Martin, 17, says: 'There was this long period of time where I was totally unco-ordinated. I'd grown but I couldn't get used to my new size and I kept bumping into things and tripping up. Not smooth at all!'*

You might think you're growing breasts! During puberty two things happen that can make boys worry they're growing breasts. The first thing is that new layers of muscle and fat develop around the chest and make it bigger. The second is that the hormone oestrogen – which occurs naturally in boys as well as girls – can make your breast tissue grow a bit. This usually goes away in boys, but it can last for up to two years. If you're concerned, talk to a doctor.

***You get body hair*** Testosterone – the male sex hormone – is what's making you break out in body hair. The hair can appear anywhere, but you'll probably notice it the most under your arms, on your legs and on the backs of your hands. It often arrives on your chest a bit later, but some boys are hairier than others and it's just as normal to end up with a hairless chest (forever) as it is to have a hairy one. You'll also start getting hair on your face. At first it's pretty wispy (bumfluff!) but it'll start getting thicker and more noticeable as time passes.

### how to wet shave

- Wash your face in warm water.
- Put on some shaving foam (or gel). It lathers up so you don't need to use much.
- Using a sharp razor, move the blade across your face in the same direction as the hair grows (usually downwards on your face and upwards on your neck).
- Rinse your razor thoroughly.
- Rinse your face with warm water.

When you use an electric razor you dry shave. It's quicker but it can be rough on your face.

**Your voice breaks** During puberty your larynx (voice box) changes shape and makes your voice get deeper. This process is what people mean when they talk about your voice 'breaking'. It can happen suddenly or you might have to go for months with your voice being high one minute and a low rumble the next.

**You get sweaty** Once you hit puberty your body starts to produce more sweat. Just keep on washing!

### Your genitals (penis and testes) grow

→ **Your testicles (or balls) get bigger.**
Testicles hang away from the body so that they're kept cool. That's because testicles are responsible for producing sperm (male sex cells) and sperm is produced at a cooler temperature than the normal body temperature of 37°C.

→ **Your scrotum (the pouch of skin that contains your testicles) starts to look darker and gets tougher.**

→ **You get pubic hair.**
This starts off being quite fine but gradually it gets thicker and coarser and there's much more of it.

→ **Your penis starts to grow.**
At first it just gets longer and then it starts getting wider. Most penises end up being about 12–18 cm long when they're erect. When they're limp they're smaller and the average size is 5–8 cm.

### THE PENIS

*Errol, 17, says: 'I was quite shocked the first time I had a wet dream. I woke up and there was sticky cum all over my pyjamas – before then I hadn't even realised I could orgasm in my sleep!'*

*Simon, 21, says: 'I had to be circumcised when I was nineteen because my foreskin was too tight and when I had an erection it was really painful. I didn't go to the doctor for ages – I was too embarrassed. But finally my girlfriend got fed up with me and insisted I did something about it. It wasn't pleasant but I'm so glad I had it done now. It means I've finally been able to have sex!'*

*Andy, 15, says: 'Everyone worries that their cock isn't long enough and it doesn't help when girls make jokes and wiggle their little fingers. It's not like anyone's going to suggest we should all whip them out and compare.'*

Penises come in all shapes and sizes. Some are short, some are long, some are fat, some are thin. There are no bones or muscles in a penis so normally it hangs flaccid (limp). The average length of a limp penis is 5–8 cm.

Some penises are circumcised. This means that the foreskin (the skin that covers the head of the penis) has been removed. People are circumcised for religious or for health reasons, but the operation doesn't affect the size of someone's penis and it doesn't lead to problems when they masturbate or have sex.

Penises enlarge and become rigid when you get an erection. They might look straight or they might bend a bit to one side but both these things are normal. But if it hurts when you get an erection – or if your penis doesn't point upwards when it happens – you need to get it checked out.

### What's an erection?

An erection happens when blood rushes into the penis and makes it stiff. The penis rises upwards but the blood stays in place because muscles at the base of the penis tighten up and trap it there.

Erections often happen when you get turned on but they can also happen for no reason at all – and can pop up at really awkward moments. There are two ways to get rid of them. One is to let your erection fade away of its own accord (you could try to help it on its way by thinking about very un-sexy things). The other way is to ejaculate (orgasm and release semen from the penis).

### What's semen?

Semen is the creamy-looking liquid that comes out of the penis and contains sperm. It comes out when you orgasm (hit the sexual climax). That can happen through masturbation, sex or involuntarily, as in wet dreams.

### What's a wet dream?

A wet dream is when you ejaculate during your sleep. You can wake up feeling wet and sticky and not realise what's happened. Wet dreams just happen – there's nothing you can do to stop them.

### *Take care of your penis!*

→ If you're uncircumcised (have a foreskin) remember that when you wash you need to pull back your foreskin and clean underneath it. If you don't then smegma (a white substance that can look and smell cheesy) will build up there and start to smell.

→ If you're uncircumcised pull back your foreskin from the head of your penis when you pee. This will stop urine getting trapped underneath it and starting to smell.

→ Go and see a doctor if you get:
  • A rash on your penis.
  • Blood coming out of your penis or blood in your semen.
  • Unusual discharge (fluid) coming out of your penis.
  • Pain when you pee.
  • If you're sexually active go and see your doctor if you get spots on your penis. Don't pick or squeeze penis spots because that can lead to infection.

### *Take care of your testes!*

→ Go and see a doctor if:
  • You get injured in your genitals and you're still in pain an hour later.
  • You get pain in your genitals for no reason.
  • You find a lump in one of your testicles.
  • One of your testicles is gradually growing bigger.

→ Getting kicked or hit in your testicles is always going to be painful, but if you're still in pain an hour later you need to see a doctor. You could have an internal injury.

→ Sometimes testicles can become twisted. This is really painful and it can damage the testicle because the blood supply is being cut off. Go to a hospital as soon as possible.

→ Testicular cancer can affect men of any age. If it's found early there's a very good chance of survival, so it's important to check yourself regularly for lumps. If you find a lump in your testicles go and see the doctor. It might be a harmless cyst (a sac filled with liquid) but it might be an early warning sign of cancer.

→ Check your testicles regularly:

- Get in a warm bath.

- Using the palms of your hands, hold your testicles and get used to the way they feel and their size. Typically, one testicle will be larger than the other and hang lower down.

- Your testicles should be smooth round the bottom and sides. At the top it will feel different because that's where it joins the tube that carries the sperm.

- Use a mirror to double-check for lumps.

# GIRLS' BODS

*Cleo, 18, says: 'Between eleven and twelve I just grew. At the start of secondary school I was tall for my year but not weirdly tall. But by the start of Year 8, I was a giant! I've got a load of stretchmarks running up my back where my growing stretched the skin – they used to look like I'd just been whipped! Luckily they've faded now and they aren't as noticeable.'*

*Michelle, 14, says: 'Me and my mate Kelly started our periods last year. We always talk about everything but I started before her and it was a bit embarrassing telling her about it. But then she came on a month later and now we get to moan together about period pain.'*

*Siobhan, 14, says: 'I'm flat-chested and I hate it. The boys say I'm really a man and none of them fancy me. My friends say I should be pleased 'cos breasts get in the way and it means I don't have problems when I play sport but I wish they'd shut up. They don't know what it's like and they sound really patronising.'*

Some people's bodies start hitting puberty when they're as young as eight – and in some people changes are still occurring when they're in their twenties. But if you get to seventeen and you aren't showing any signs of puberty (you've had no breast growth, periods or body hair) then it's a good idea to go and see your doctor to make sure there aren't any problems.

## SO WHAT CHANGES DURING PUBERTY?

### You change shape

Often the first bit of you to get bigger is your feet – and that can make you feel a bit clumsy until you get used to their new size. Then, as you grow upwards, your hips start to get larger, your boobs develop and your body starts to curve in towards the waist. Everyone goes through these changes at a different speed, so don't worry if you look different to your mates. Talk to your doctor if there's something that's really bothering you.

*Aisha, 13, says: 'I've started my periods and I'm a 36C cup bra but I'm not growing taller – I'm just getting fatter. My sister says it's puppy fat and when I grow it will disappear 'cos that's what happened to her ...*

## You get body hair

During puberty you'll start to find hair appearing in the pubic region (around your vagina), under your arms and on your legs.

But hair doesn't necessarily stop there! It's totally normal for girls to get hair anywhere on their body, including on their face, and it can sprout up at any age. Everyone's different, so you might get hair somewhere – like above your lip or on your chin or across your belly or on your toes – while your mates don't. It's not a big deal and if you don't like it you can get rid of it.

### How to get rid of unwanted hair

There are various methods of hair removal for different parts of your body:

**Shaving:** People usually shave their legs and under their arms. Hairs grow back quickly so you might end up wanting to shave once a day. You use a razor with a sharp blade to cut the hair off at the skin. Wash the skin in warm water, lather on some shaving foam or gel and run the razor across the skin in the same direction as the hair grows. Then rinse the skin clean.

You can either buy disposable razors or buy one razor and replace the blade regularly. You'll find them at the chemists along with shaving cream or gel. The shaving cream helps to moisturise your skin and to prevent cuts. Soap is harsher on your skin. Different shaving creams are made for men and women (they work the same way but they smell different).

**Waxing:** People usually wax their legs and their bikini line (the bikini line is the area around the edge of your bikini bottoms – so if you wax your bikini line then when you wear your bikini no hair will be showing). Warm wax gets smoothed on to the skin, it dries and gets attached to the hairs, and then it's pulled off – ripping the hairs out with it. It can hurt a bit but the hair stays gone for longer than it would if you shaved.

**Bleaching:** People bleach their facial hair. Bleaching is putting chemicals on the hair to make it lighter and less noticeable. Be careful if you're doing this, because the chemicals might irritate your skin. Test out the bleach on a tiny area of skin first.

**Depilatory Creams:** People use creams on their legs, on their bikini lines and even on their facial hair. The cream gets smoothed on for a recommended length of time. When it's removed the hair comes off with it. Depilatory creams can irritate the skin, so always test them on a tiny area first and never leave them on for longer than the recommended time. You can buy hair-removal products in chemists and supermarkets or you can go to a beauty salon and have hair removed professionally.

*Katie, 14, says: 'Mum always said I wasn't allowed to shave my legs 'cos if I did the hair would grow back thicker and more noticeable. At first she really put me off the whole idea but then I figured even if the hair did come back thicker I could just shave it off again. It's not going to get so bushy I can't get a razor through it!'*

## You start having periods

Your periods are the result of changes going on inside your body. Girls have two ovaries in their bodies and inside these are thousands of tiny eggs. When sperm meets one of these eggs, pregnancy can occur.

But for that to happen the egg has to be in the right place. So, once a girl's body is mature enough, every month hormones stimulate the release of one egg into a girl's Fallopian tubes. These tubes join the ovaries to the uterus (the part of the body where a baby would develop). While the egg is travelling along the Fallopian tube the lining of the uterus starts to get thicker – so that if the egg is fertilised by a sperm while it's in the fallopian tubes, the uterus will be in the right condition to nourish it when it arrives.

Usually, however, the egg arrives in the uterus without meeting a sperm and that means the thick lining isn't needed. So it starts to break down and the mixture of lining and blood and egg gets washed out of the body.

This is called menstruating – or having a period.

*How long do periods last?* Periods can last for anything from two to eight days and they can happen as often as every three weeks, or be up to five weeks apart. The first few times you have your period it might be very light – just a few spots of blood. Don't worry about the colour either. The blood might look brown or red depending on how fresh it is – how fast it's being washed out of your body.

When you first start having periods they don't always come regularly – but after a few months you should start being able to estimate when you're going to be on and stock up on tampons or sanitary towels.

*What's better – tampons or towels?* Most girls use either tampons or sanitary towels (pads) when they've got their periods. The towels are pieces of absorbent material that are shaped to stick inside your knickers, while tampons are cylindrical pieces of cotton that you insert into your vagina to soak up the blood. Whatever you use, you need to make sure you change it every few hours.

Using towels is simple, but tampons can be tricky until you're used to them. The easiest ones to use are applicator tampons, because the applicator helps to push the tampon up into your vagina.

Here's what you do:

→ Relax. If you're tense it will be harder to put the tampon in.

→ Take the tampon out of its wrapper. The bit where the cord's hanging down is the bottom of the tampon.

→ Hold the tampon in the middle, just above where the two tubes join, with the cord at the bottom.

→ Put the top of the tampon into your vagina. It needs to be angled so it's facing slightly towards your back.

→ Insert the tampon a little way into your vagina. It should feel comfortable. If it doesn't it's probably not at the right angle, so try moving it around to find the position it should be in.

→ When it feels comfortable, hold on to the outside tube of the applicator and push the inner tube inside. This inserts the tampon into your vagina.

→ Now pull both tubes out of your body. The tampon will be left behind with the cord hanging out of your vagina. When you want to remove it, all you have to do is tug the cord gently. You should change your tampon every four to eight hours – and definitely don't leave it in for longer than eight hours.

## Toxic Shock Syndrome

Toxic Shock Syndrome (TSS) is a very rare illness. A bacteria that lives in the nose and vagina can sometimes release toxins that poison the body. This can be triggered by insect bites, infected wounds, burns or through tampon use. The symptoms might include dizziness, vomiting or a rash. If you think you've got TSS, remove your tampon and go straight to a doctor or to a hospital.

***What's period pain?*** When you have your period, muscles inside you relax and contract to move the blood and uterine lining out of your body. These muscle contractions are the things that can cause period pain. Not everyone gets it, and some people only get it mildly, but some people find their periods really painful. There are things you can do to ease the pain:

→ You can take painkillers (but don't exceed the recommended dose).
→ You can exercise.
→ You can drink peppermint tea.
→ You can take a warm bath.
→ You can put a hot-water bottle on your stomach or back.

But if your pains are still unbearable, go and see your doctor. They might be able to prescribe you something that will work for you.

***How do you feel when you've got your period?*** Everyone reacts differently to their periods – and you can even react differently from one period to the next. But at this time of the month your hormones are at their lowest level and this can result in some weird behaviour – especially in the days leading up to your period. This behaviour is called PMS, premenstrual syndrome ...

*Charlie, 14, says: 'I get really emotional just before I start my period. I'll start crying over nothing and feel really sorry for myself – even if I don't have any reason to! If something bad is going on in my life then I'm even worse – I'll spend the whole night crying about it. I know it's my hormones but that doesn't make the feelings go away.'*

*Wendy, 16, says: 'My boyfriend avoids me at that time of the month. He says when I'm about to have my period I get really moody and I deliberately try to start fights. At first I couldn't understand why we were fighting 'cos normally I never fight but then I put two and two together and realised it must be that I was getting PMT (premenstrual tension). I'd heard about it but I didn't know what it was. Now I do know I just apologise in advance!'*

Lots of girls get depressed or tense or moody when they've got PMS – and things that normally wouldn't bother them can really *get on their nerves. The fact that their hormones are going crazy isn't helped by the other symptoms of PMS either. PMS can:*

→ Make you break out in spots.
→ Give you sore breasts that feel swollen and tender.
→ Make you tired and headachy.
→ Make you feel bloated. Your body retains more water when you've got your period, so you feel heavy and your stomach sticks out more than normal.

## Period problems

If you get any of the following symptoms, go and check them out with your doctor:

→ Your periods stop. (If you're having sex, this might be a sign you're pregnant, so go and do a pregnancy test.)

→ You're getting stomach cramps that are too painful to cope with.

→ You're bleeding so much you need to change your tampon or towel about once an hour.

→ Your period is still heavy after seven days.

→ Your periods have become really irregular. (It's normal for periods to be irregular for the first year or so, but after that they should start coming at fairly regular intervals.)

→ You're finding spots of blood in your knickers – but it's not period blood.

## You start growing breasts

*Helen, 13, says: 'Oh. My. God. I did not want these enormous things on my chest. Even when I'm harnessed into my bra I still feel like they're bouncing along ahead of me. I don't feel like a real person any more – I feel like a giant pair of breasts.'*

*Saskia, 15, says: 'I don't know what the big deal about breasts is. They're just there. I don't waste time obsessing about mine.'*

Breasts come in all shapes and sizes. One might be bigger than the other, your nipples might stick in or out, you might get hairs growing on your breasts, your areolas (the coloured area of skin around the nipple) might be brown or pink or purplish ...

Whatever you've got, be proud of 'em. If you like your breasts, other people will too!

→ The first thing you'll notice when your breasts start to grow is that your areolas and your nipples start to get bigger. They might start to ache a bit too.

→ Your breasts are mounds of fatty tissue that protect the milk glands and ducts that women need to feed their babies. As the milk glands start to grow, fat tissue starts to build. At first this just feels like a lump behind your nipple and sometimes it happens in one breast before the other. Don't worry that you're only developing on one side – the other one will catch up!

→ Gradually, the fatty tissue fills out and becomes more rounded and you'll need to start wearing a bra. If you go to a bra shop, they'll measure you and make sure you get one that's the right size.

*Take care of your breasts!* You need to keep an eye out for lumps in your breasts, because in very rare cases they can be a sign of breast cancer. Breast cancer is very, *very* unusual in teenagers, but it's always worth getting unusual lumps checked out by your doctor:

→ Examine your breasts once a month, just after your period finishes.

→ Lie down and put a pillow behind one shoulder. Then raise that arm and put it behind your head.

→ Using your other hand, check the raised breast by pressing around it in a circle and making sure there aren't any lumps.

→ Repeat the same steps on the other breast.

→ Use a mirror to do a final visual check for changes in your breast.

## EVERYBODY'S BODS

There are things that happen to everyone during puberty, regardless of what sex they are. Like spots ...

### *SPOTS*

Acne, pimples, zits ... whatever you call them, spots are a pain in the bum (and sometimes they're a pain on the bum). You start getting them because your skin's reacting to all the hormones flying around inside your body, and they can pop up anywhere. OK, so they're most visible when they're on your face, but plenty of people have spotty backs, spotty chests or spotty shoulders – you're not the only one!

### Does anything make spots worse?

→ **Wearing a lot of make-up can make spots worse. That doesn't mean you should never cover up, but always cleanse your skin before you go to sleep.**

→ **Stress can make spots pop up and, unfortunately, that can just make your stress worse. But once the stress is over, the spots will die down.**

→ **Getting hot and sweaty can aggravate your spots.**

→ **For girls, spots can get worse just before their period because their hormone levels increase.**

### So how do you get rid of them?

Spots do disappear but it takes time. Most people start off by trying 'natural' remedies like cutting out chocolate. The idea behind the chocolate ban is that greasy foods are bad for your skin. Most doctors don't agree with this – they reckon what you eat doesn't really affect your skin. Still, it's not a bad idea to look after it – and whether or not chocolate has an effect, drinking lots of water is a definite skin bonus.

Then there are the creams, lotions and potions you can buy in the chemists. These work for some people but they can make other people's skin feel dry, sore or itchy. They come in different strengths so always go for the mildest first, see how your skin reacts and, if you think you need to, build up the strength. (The strength is written on the label and the mildest is usually 2.5%.)

But if you've been trying natural remedies or over-the-counter potions for two months and they haven't made a difference, then go to see your doctor. They might be able to prescribe you antibiotics or creams that will work for you.

### Should I squeeze them?

The danger with squeezing spots is that you force all the oil and bacteria deeper into your face. Picking at spots can also leave scars that stick around forever. If you've ever seen anyone with lots of little pits in their face, then that's probably acne scarring.

But some spots you can squeeze. Here are the rules:

→ **If the spot is red or white – DON'T SQUEEZE.**

→ **If the spot is green – DON'T SQUEEZE and go to see your doctor. Green spots aren't normal.**

→ **If the spot starts to bleed when you squeeze – STOP.**

→ **If your spot is topped off by a yellow or a black head, then you can squeeze it. Wash your hands first. Then start to squeeze (using your thumb and finger – not your nails). When all the yellow/black muckiness is gone, dab your spot with antiseptic, wash your hands and leave the rest of the spot alone and let it heal.**

### But they're making me really miserable

Spots can make people feel really depressed. They get embarrassed about the way they look, they think that no one will fancy them because they have spots, and there are always some idiots around who think it's funny to comment on spots.

The thing is, spots do go. The other thing is that you are a lot more than just your spots and anyone who's worth talking to will know that. The fact you have spots isn't going to stop you having a social life – the thing that will stop you having a social life is the way you *think* people are going to respond to you. But you need to give them some credit. Would you dismiss someone because they had zits? No, you wouldn't. What's more – pretty much everyone knows what it's like to have spots or to have something that they're embarrassed about. Don't put your life on hold just because your oil glands are going mental - you *really* don't need to.

## HORMONES

But the changes going on during puberty don't just show up in your physical appearance. The hormones rampaging around inside you can send you off on an emotional roller-coaster ride. That might just mean that your sex drive kicks in and you start fancying the pants off your teachers/ your mates/ anyone who's ever been in a Hollywood film, but for a lot of people puberty can bring with it some really destructive emotions.

You might start being really badly affected by feelings of depression, anger, jealousy, frustration, self-loathing or hate without really understanding where those feelings are coming from. Or maybe you've got reasons to feel bad but your hormones are making those emotions even more intense.

If you're feeling messed up and you don't know how to deal with it, then *please* find someone you trust to talk to. In lots of ways it's easier to talk to your mates, but if there are any adults you feel close to, often they're the ones who can help the most. They might not have gone through exactly what you're going through, but they'll have had things happen to them in their lives and they've come through it. They know how hard it can be.

If you're feeling bad remember that during puberty your hormones go wild. That's at least part of what's making you feel bad. Hang on in there.

## 2 SEX

Sometimes it seems that as soon as you become a teenager you're supposed to be obsessed with sex. But people start getting sexual and romantic feelings at different times. Your mates might be ogling every girl that walks by; while all you want to do is talk video games. If sex isn't a big deal for you at the moment, don't worry about it. Your sex drive might not have kicked in yet, or you might be someone who needs more stimulation than other people to feel turned on.

*Karina, 14, says: 'I think it's sad the way sex is such a big deal. You turn on the TV or you open a magazine and it's sex, sex, sex. No wonder so many teenagers feel like they have to do it so quickly.'*

*Tyra, 13, says: 'My friends talk about which celebrities they fancy but I don't really get what they mean. How can they fancy someone they don't know? I think those people are good-looking but I don't feel anything else about them.'*

*Oliver, 15, says: 'Girls aren't one of my priorities at the moment. I want to spend my spare time writing music and doing stuff with my band.'*

But for other people sexual feelings are a huge part of hitting puberty. The truckloads of hormones racing round their bodies are affecting the way they feel about themselves, about other people, about themselves with other people ...

*Annabel, 18, says: 'When I was thirteen I had this crush on my Geography teacher. She was a woman so I didn't say anything to anyone about it 'cos I was worried it meant I was a lesbian. It wasn't really sexual – I just used to make up these little scenarios where she'd be hugging me or looking after me. But, I guess I was having sexual feelings for her in a way.'*

*Duncan, 17, says: 'I started kissing girls – using tongues! – when I was at primary school. I can't remember a time when I wasn't interested in girls to be honest. My brother's ten years older than me and he used to go out with this girl who was always round at our house. I was forever cuddling up to her and trying to get near her boobs. I can't have been more than about nine or ten but even then I thought breasts were the greatest things ever.'*

*Gary, 17, says: 'I used to spend my whole time fantasising what it would be like to have my crush touch me. I almost walked into a post box once 'cos I was so busy dreaming about it.'*

*Rachel, 14, says: 'My friends and I are boy-obsessed. There's this one really fit boy who gets our bus and we've started stalking him to find out where he lives. Then we sit in class talking about him and making up ways to make him fancy us.'*

When you have sexual feelings, your body responds to them and gets turned on (sexually aroused). Sometimes this can feel really noticeable – like when a boy gets an erection – but sometimes the changes can be so subtle you're not even aware of them happening. The pupils in your eyes can get bigger, your heartbeat can speed up, your temperature can increase ...

## SO WHAT TURNS PEOPLE ON?

Everyone finds different things attractive. From the amount of fuss that's made about Page 3 girls (the topless girls in the newspaper) you'd think the only thing boys want from a girl is big boobs. OK, so some of them do – but some of them don't. Naked bodies are only one of a whole load of things that turn people on...

People can get turned on by things they see ...

*Francisco, 16, says: 'I think it's really sexy when you see someone doing something they're good at. I fell in love with this girl once when I saw her in the school play. She was so talented she blew me away.'*

*Jack, 15, says: 'I like girls with dimples.'*

*Verity, 15, says: 'If a boy makes eye contact with me and smiles it makes me feel something for him. It's weird – it just makes my heart jump a little.'*

Or by something they hear ...

*Leo, 18, says: 'I get horny when I hear ice-cream vans! That* sounds really dumb doesn't it?! But it's true. It reminds me of last summer and hanging out with my girlfriend in the park.'

*Laura, 15, says:* 'Boys with deep voices get me. It's SO sexy when a boy sounds like a man.'

Or by something they smell ...

*Chrissie, 17, says:* 'If I smell someone wearing DKNY For Men I want to rush after them! It's amazing.'

*Ben, 18, says:* 'I think leather smells sexy. I've just bought myself a leather jacket so I smell sexy now!'

Or by the way something feels ...

*Abigail, 16, says:* 'I was at a party once and this boy came up behind me and lifted the hair off the back of my neck. Then he kissed me right down the back of my shoulders. It felt unbelievable.'

*James, 19, says:* 'My girlfriend's got this soft jumper that she wraps herself up in. It's really strokeable – I love the way her body feels inside it.'

Or by something they taste ...

*Matt, 18, says:* 'I like the taste of a girl's mouth when she's just done her teeth. It makes my tongue tingle!'

A lot of people spend a *lot* of time discussing who they fancy and who they reckon has sex appeal. But the thing about sexual attraction is that it's completely personal. What one person thinks is knee-meltingly, stomach-churningly sexy someone else doesn't even notice ...

*Tom, 17, says:* 'My ideal woman is someone with long slim legs and blonde hair. I prefer it if they're shorter than me but I don't want someone who's so short they look like a child.'

*Joe, 16, says:* 'I like brunettes. J-Lo will do!'

*Gail, 16, says:* 'I go for boys who can make me laugh. It's a bonus if they're cute – but the most important thing is their personality.'

*Helen, 15, says:* 'I'd never go out with an ugly guy. I don't care how clever or funny or nice they are – I'd be friends with someone like that but I wouldn't want to date them. I like guys with dark hair and bright green or blue eyes. Oh, and long eyelashes!'

*John, 16, says: 'All my girlfriends have looked really different but they've all had really nice smiles. A good smile goes a long way!'*

When it comes to deciding who's sexy you can't rely on your mates – you've got to follow your own instincts or you could end up missing out on someone special.

*Dom, 18, says: 'I almost prefer girls if my mates aren't big on them. To me that means they're individuals and it might be that I bring out something special in them that no one else does.'*

*Reba, 16, says: 'I admit I do listen to my mates' opinions a bit too much. I hope I wouldn't dump someone just 'cos my friends didn't rate him but if I'm honest it probably would make me think less of him.'*

*Iowa, 17, says: 'When I was younger what my mates thought was a big deal 'cos I wanted to fit in. Now I let them have their opinions but I think for myself. It would be disastrous if we all listened to each other anyway – we'd all end up going after the same boys!'*

Sexiness isn't just about looking a certain way, it's about the whole person – their personality, their sense of humour, the way they feel about themselves. Often the sexiest people are just the people who like who they are and are relaxed to be around.

But there's a big difference between liking or loving someone and being sexually attracted to them. Sexual attraction is all about wanting physical contact. That can be confusing if you end up feeling sexually attracted to people you've got nothing in common with – or people you don't even like.

However hard it is, it's a good idea to try and let your head rule your body and not your body rule your head. Don't get involved with someone until you know them and you're sure it's something *you* want to do.

*Emily, 15, says: 'In school it's like there's a divide between the people who say they've had sex and the people who haven't. It's like if you have you're suddenly more grown-up and sophisticated than everyone else. But I don't want to have sex until I meet someone I fall in love with.'*

There are lots of levels of getting sexual with someone.

Never go further than you feel comfortable going – and never try to make someone else go somewhere they don't want to go. Pressuring someone into doing something – or feeling pressured to do something is *wrong*. Good sexual experiences are all about trusting someone and *wanting* to explore their body and have them explore yours.

You should never wind up feeling:

→ **Used**
→ **Guilty**
→ **Ashamed**

If you don't want to do something you don't have to do it. If someone tries to make you do something you don't want to do, they're only thinking about themselves. Why should you do anything for someone like that?

Respect yourself. It's your body. You're allowed to wait until the time is right for you.

### sex and the law

| | |
|---|---|
| • In England, Wales and Scotland it's illegal to have sex when you're under sixteen. | • In Northern Ireland it's illegal to have sex when you're under seventeen. |

## MASTURBATION

*'Don't knock masturbation. It's sex with someone you love.'*

**Woody Allen**

Masturbating means touching your genitals and turning yourself on. It's forbidden in some religions and cultures but, if you are allowed to do it, it's a good way of finding out about your own body and what you like – and it's fun! In the old days people used to think masturbation was dangerous and they invented a whole lot of lies about what happened when you masturbated ...

**Ye olde lie # 1:**   **People who masturbate go blind.**
**Ye olde lie # 2:**   **People who masturbate go mad.**

Ye olde lie # 3:     If a boy masturbates his penis will fall off.

Ye olde lie # 4:     People who masturbate go bald.

Ye olde lie # 5:     People who masturbate get hairs growing on the palms of their hands.

Er – no! None of those things would happen to you because you masturbated. If you want to masturbate, go ahead and enjoy it.

*Will, 17, says: 'I was about ten when I discovered that touching my dick was fun. But I can't really describe it as masturbating – it was more kind of fumbling around.'*

*Jess, 16, says: 'My friend told me she got turned on by those water jet things you get in some baths and swimming pools. So I tried that and it worked! Sometimes I can get turned on when I'm cycling too – but it's only when I sit on the bike a certain way and I can't always get it.'*

*Angela, 17, says: 'Sometimes when I wake up I'm lying on my front and moving my body up and down the bed and I feel like I'm about to come. It's great!'*

People find their own techniques for masturbating, but for boys it usually involves grasping the penis and moving their hand up and down, changing the speed and pressure until they ejaculate (semen comes out of the tip of the penis).

For girls it usually involves touching their clitoris – a little bump at the top of the vagina that's *really* sensitive to touch. They rub or stroke the clitoris and can turn themselves on so much that they have an orgasm. An orgasm is basically the peak of sex – when all the sensations build up into a climax of feelings.

It's not just single people who masturbate; people still masturbate when they're going out with someone and some of them love watching their girlfriend or boyfriend masturbating in front of them.

There are only three things to remember about masturbation:

→ Don't masturbate in public – it's illegal to do that.

→ Be careful if you stick something inside you when you masturbate, (e.g. a sex toy) because if it's not clean it could give you an infection.

→ If you're masturbating a lot and your genitals start to feel sore
– take a rest. You can have too much of a good thing!

# SEXUAL ORIENTATION

One of the things that can be most confusing about the
whole sex issue is working out your own sexual identity.

Most people would describe themselves as either:

→ **Heterosexual or 'straight':**

   People who are heterosexual are mainly attracted to people
   of the opposite sex. So boys fancy girls and girls fancy boys.

→ **Bisexual:**

   People who are bisexual are strongly attracted to people of
   either sex, boys and girls.

→ **Homosexual – gay or lesbian:**

   People who are homosexual are mainly attracted to people of
   the same sex. Boys fancy boys and girls fancy girls.

For a lot of people sexual identity is something they want to
explore. It's not as simple as knowing that they're 'gay' or
'straight' – they feel a lot of emotions and they're trying to
work them out.

*Emma, 18, says: 'When I was younger I used to have a crush on a
girl in the year above. I used to imagine what it would be like to
kiss her. I'm really into boys now and I'm pretty sure I'm straight
but I did think I might be a lesbian for a while.'*

*Ziggy, 17, says: 'I fancy girls but the only people I've ever fallen in
love with are boys. But I've been out with girls and I've never even
kissed a boy. So I don't know if I'm straight or if I'm bisexual or if
I'm gay. I want to kiss a boy and see what it's like. Maybe that would
help me work it out.'*

*Camilla, 17, says: 'I've snogged girls before but it's only ever been
as a dare and it doesn't turn me on. I wouldn't want to go any
further with any of them.'*

*Nick, 19, says: 'I'm straight. I've never had to question that. I've never met a bloke that I'd find even remotely fanciable – but I've met thousands of women that I'd happily shag!'*

*Sean, 19, says: 'It took me ages to admit to myself that I might be gay. I had a lot of stuff going on at home when I was younger and I just focused on that instead of thinking about sex. It wasn't until I left home when I was eighteen to go on a gap year that I started to realise that I did have sexual feelings – and they weren't for girls ...'*

It can be hard for people to explore their feelings about sexuality if they think they might be bisexual or homosexual. To start with they might not be sure of what they're feeling – or why they're feeling that way. Then they've got to deal with worrying that they're 'wrong' to feel the way they do. And on top of that it's easy to worry about the way other people are going to react ...

*Rob, 21, says: 'I didn't want to be gay – I wanted to be straight. I wanted to be the perfect son and go to university and get a good job and have children. All through school I was really sporty and I got good grades and I chatted up girls ... but at the back of my mind there was always this feeling that I wasn't being myself or that there was something different about me. Then, when I was eighteen, I met this other boy and I fell in love with him. Nothing ever happened and I think he would have run screaming if I'd told him how I felt but it forced me to admit to myself that there was more to me than I wanted there to be. But I still haven't done much about it. I've discussed it with a couple of my closest friends but I haven't told anyone else – or my parents. I guess I'm afraid that I'd lose them or they'd think everything about me was a lie. I feel a bit as though it is. I'm just hoping that as time goes by it'll all start getting easier ...'*

*James, 18, says: 'I'm very open about my sexuality but I know that there are people out there who will hate me because of it – even though they don't know a thing about me. Slowly, the culture's changing but I think there'll always be homophobia – just like there'll probably always be sexism and racism.'*

*Tess, 19, says: 'I'm a lesbian. That makes me part of a minority group. I don't think your sexual orientation should make any difference to the way people act towards you but sometimes it does. I don't mean that people are necessarily different towards you but sometimes I feel like any girl I meet expects me to try and snog her. I get bored of explaining that just 'cos I fancy girls doesn't mean I fancy every girl.'*

## HOMOPHOBIA

Homophobia means being afraid of, or hating, homosexuals. It's sad but it's true that some people can be prejudiced against other people just because of who they're attracted to. That's hard to deal with and it doesn't help when words like 'gay' are used as a way of putting people down.

But it's not like it's 'right' to be straight and 'wrong' to be gay – they're just different. If other people can't accept that, that's their problem.

That doesn't mean that prejudice isn't upsetting, and if you're feeling lonely or isolated it can help to talk to other people who've experienced what you're going through. If you ring one of the groups listed in the contacts section – like the Gay and Lesbian Switchboard – they'll be able to put you in touch with lesbian or gay people in your area.

*Damon, 20, says: 'I grew up in a tiny village in the middle of nowhere and I didn't know anyone who was gay. That made it even weirder when I started thinking I might be. I wanted to talk to someone about how I was feeling but I didn't know how to start going about getting in touch with someone. I didn't want to go on to a gay chat room 'cos I didn't want to date someone; I just wanted to get my head round it all. But I was scared of what other gay people were like too. The only image of a gay person I had was this stereotypical image of someone really camp who liked wearing things like tight white tops and leather caps.*

*In the end it wasn't until I left college and went to university in Leeds that I started to find out stuff. I joined a gay society and met people through it who'd been out for a while and it got rid of a lot of my preconceptions. You don't have to act in a certain way to be gay. It would be easy to mistake a lot of gay people as straight if you didn't know them – they're not different or outrageous – they're just into something different sexually.*

*Now I even know that a couple of other people from my village school are gay too! We were all there worrying about it and we never worked it out about each other. I wish I had known – it would have made being a teenager a lot easier.'*

## COMING OUT

It can take a long time before people feel ready to tell others that they're homosexual. They may have been intimidated by people making homophobic comments – or they might have wanted to come to terms with their own sexuality before they face other people's reactions.

Telling other people you're gay is nicknamed 'coming out'. Remember, it's up to you who you come out to – and when – and you've got to be prepared for getting a whole range of responses ...

*Tom, 17, says: 'The first person I told just shrugged and said they'd already guessed. I didn't know whether to be relieved that they weren't bothered or worried that everyone already knew about me.'*

*Kate, 16, says: 'I told my best friend that I was gay. The thing was that I had feelings for her and I think she might have picked up on that. She was shocked to start with and didn't say much. It didn't change our friendship but she did keep going on about boys and made it very clear that she'd never felt that way for me.'*

*Jay, 18, says: 'My mum guessed and confronted me about it. I didn't want to lie so I told her the truth and then went to give her a big hug. It was really awkward but she tried her best to be cool. She just said, "Make sure you're careful", and sort of hugged me back.'*

*David, 18, says: 'My dad won't accept I'm gay. When I told him, he wouldn't talk and wouldn't go near me. Then he got angry and now he just keeps telling my mum that it's a phase I'm going through and that I'm rebelling. It's making me really angry but I don't know what to say to him.'*

*Kelly, 19, says: 'No one said anything to my face when I came out but I know some people started talking about me behind my back. But then a lot of other people were a lot more supportive than I expected them to be. On balance I'm really glad I came out.'*

You're under no obligation to tell anyone about your sexuality. Come out when you want to and only come out to the people you want to know. Getting a bad reaction from someone you're close to can be devastating, and you need to have come to terms with who you are yourself before trying to cope with that.

Having said that, a lot of people feel very relieved when they tell people the truth. Being honest about their feelings allows them to express who they are and live the way they want to live.

### TRANSSEXUALS

A transsexual is someone who believes that they were born the wrong sex – so girls feel like they're actually boys and boys feel that, although they have a penis, they're girls.

It can be really difficult to deal with this, and a lot of transsexuals can feel desperately unhappy and confused about their identities. If they want to, and if they can convince a doctor that they really need to, transsexuals can undergo operations and hormone therapy that will turn them into the sex they believe they should be.

Don't confuse transsexuals with transvestites – a transvestite is someone who likes to dress up in clothes that are normally worn by the opposite sex. Transsexuals might do this, but that's to do with expressing what they see as their real identity, whereas transvestites just like wearing the clothes. People think that if you're a transvestite you're gay, but transvestites can be heterosexual *or* homosexual.

## GETTING LIPPY

Whatever you're into – boys, girls, boys and girls – it's kind of likely that the first sexual thing you'll get up to is kissing. OK, so not all kisses are sexy. Giving your gran a peck on the cheek definitely isn't – and neither are 'It-girly' air kisses. Proper, sexy kissing is a bit more intimate (we're talking saliva-swapping here). When people use their tongues to kiss they call it French kissing, but proper lippy sessions are

also known as snogging, smooching, getting off, necking ...
Whatever you call it, good kissing can take a bit of practice.

*Junior, 18, says: 'I used to practise my kissing technique on my mirror. That wasn't because I fancied myself! I just wanted to be able to see what I was doing. One time I caught my little brother practising too – he'd drawn a pair of lips on his hand and he was slobbering all over them!'*

Kissing styles do vary – and people like different things – but some are, uh, better than others ...

*Tammy, 17, says: 'One boy I got off with just stuck his tongue in and out of my mouth like he was a lizard or something. It was horrible.'*

*Michael, 15, says: 'I hate it when girls eat your face. Like – I don't want saliva all over my chin!'*

## KISSING CRISES

→ **Bad breath.**
If you think you might be a bit whiffy then it's time to become friends with the toothbrush – at least twice a day. If you're still paranoid, carry mints or chewing gum with you and don't smoke. That makes you smell worse.

→ **Bumping bits.**
Everyone has had a snog where they've bumped noses or teeth or missed someone's mouth completely! It happens – just smile and get back to locking lips. And don't worry about your braces getting tangled together – you'll never meet anyone that's really happened to.

→ **Height difference.**
If one of you is way taller than the other one, you'll probably get uncomfortable if you try and snog standing up. So sit down.

→ **Making the move.**
You want to go for it but you're not sure if they want it? Check out their body language. If they're leaning towards you, they're looking at you and there's a bit of a vibe going on, then you're probably in there. But if you're still uncertain, try leaning in and whispering something in their ear. It'll bring your mouths that much closer together ...

→ **Eye to eye?**
It's up to you whether or not you keep your eyes open when you snog. Some people like being able to gaze into wide-open peepers – but it can be a bit intimidating to be eyeballed while you kiss. It's your choice.

→ **Tongue in cheek.**
Snogging is not about shoving your tongue into someone's mouth and letting it lie there like a big wet slug. Start off by kissing with your lips only and then – if you want to – you can start introducing your tongue to the proceedings. The more you kiss, the more you'll develop your own style, so take the tongue slowly until you know you're doing it right.

→ **The hands.**
Travelling hands can cause problems or they can hot things up. It's your call where you put them, but to start with it's a good idea to park them around their waist or behind their necks.

# TOUCHY FEELY

Touching another person is a *big* part of sex. It doesn't have to be touching their genitals (private parts) or their nipples – caressing people pretty much anywhere on their body can feel good.

That's because people are covered in 'erogenous zones' – sensitive areas of skin where touching turns them on. Everyone's got different hot spots; some people love their hair being stroked, some go crazy when their earlobes are being nuzzled and some people have got a thing about their toes. It's not just about touching them with your fingers either – kissing or licking or blowing air across a person's body are all ways of turning them on. Whatever you do, just remember that both people have to feel comfortable and happy with it. Don't do anything that makes you feel awkward and stay aware of how the other person's reacting. If you're doing something they don't like – stop.

## BEING GROPED / FELT UP

Groping someone, or feeling them up, is usually used to describe someone touching or squeezing a girl's breasts but it can also be used for pretty much any time when someone's hands go wandering over someone else's body – especially near their nipples, genitals or bum.

## FINGERING

Fingering is the word for playing with a girl's genitals – either stroking them or inserting your fingers into her vagina. You're masturbating her, trying to sexually excite her and, if she's comfortable with it and you do stuff she likes, it probably will turn her on. But if she's not into it or you're too rough, it can just be painful and awkward.

## HAND JOBS

A hand job is when you put your hand round a boy's penis and move it up and down (at a rhythm that suits the boy) until he ejaculates (semen comes out of his penis). Just like masturbating a girl, this can be really fun for him but, if he's not comfortable with what you're doing or if you're rough, then again it can just be painful and awkward.

# ARE YOU READY FOR SEX?

If you're touching or feeling another person then your body's probably going a bit crazy and you're starting to think, 'Maybe, just maybe, this will be someone I end up having sex with'.

But being physically turned on isn't the same thing as being ready for sex. Before you go any further you need to stop and work out what your boundaries are – how far you really want all this to go. You also need to know that you'll be able to stop if it gets too heavy.

To work out if you're *really* ready to take this further you need to ask yourself the following questions ...

→ **Is this person someone I love and respect and would never regret having sex with?**

If the answer's no, then you should think very hard before you take things further.

→ **Why do I want to have sex?**

If you only want sex because your friends are boasting that they've done it or because you think you shouldn't still be a virgin – don't do it. These aren't good reasons for having sex. Loads of people lie and say they've had sex before they really have – and there's no 'right' age to lose your virginity.

→ **Am I feeling pressured to have sex?**

You should never feel pressured into doing something you don't want to do. You'll end up feeling hurt, angry and used.

→ **Am I sixteen or older – and is my partner sixteen or older (seventeen in Northern Ireland)?**

Sixteen (or seventeen in Northern Ireland) is the age when you're allowed to have sex if you want to. Until you're that age, it's illegal.

→ **Do I know how to avoid getting pregnant / getting a girl pregnant?**

If you're not clued-up about birth control, then you shouldn't be having sex.

→ **Do I know how to avoid getting a sexually transmitted infection (see page 77)?**

If you don't know how to practise safe sex and why you need to practise safe sex, you shouldn't be having sex – because it wouldn't be safe.

→ **Have you discussed sex with the other person?**

If this person is special enough to have sex with, it shouldn't be hard to talk to them about important things – like sex. You both need to feel a hundred per cent comfortable and trusting before you take things further.

→ **Does your partner love and respect you?**

If what you're feeling isn't a two-way thing, you could end up being used ...

Being ready for sex means being physically *and* emotionally ready. Be sorted – not sorry.

# ORAL SEX

Oral sex is when one person uses their mouth (lips and tongue – teeth are painful!) to suck, lick, kiss and play with another person's genitals. You can catch STIs (sexually transmitted infections) from oral sex so you need to take precautions.

Practising oral sex on a boy is called fellatio, going down, giving head or giving a blow job.

Blow jobs are a bit like hand jobs, except that instead of using your hand to stimulate the penis you use your lips, mouth and tongue. The girl wraps her lips round the penis and lets it slide up and down in her mouth. If she finds the right rhythm and keeps doing it then the boy will probably ejaculate (semen will squirt into her mouth). The girl has to decide whether to spit it out or swallow it.

Practising oral sex on a girl is called cunnilingus, going down, muff-diving or licking someone out. The boy licks, sucks and kisses the girl's vagina.

A '69' is when two people give each other oral sex at the same time. It takes a lot of co-ordination!

Some people think oral sex is even more intimate than penetrative sex. You do have to be relaxed with someone to put their genitals near your mouth – or let their mouth go near yours!

Some people worry about oral sex because they think their genitals will smell or look weird, but genitals only smell if you've got an infection or you don't wash. If you do have an infection, you've probably already smelled a bad smell and you should go and see a doctor to get it cleared up. And if you don't wash – yurk, what are you like? Go to the bathroom immediately!

Just like every other sexual activity, whether or not you engage in oral sex is your choice. You're not under any obligation to do it – even if they do it to you. You're also not under any obligation to let them do it to you if you don't want them to.

# CONTRACEPTION

*Joe, 16, says: 'When I get together with a girl I can't stop trying to take it further. I get turned on really quickly and I get so hard it hurts.'*

*Sophie, 15, says: 'I'm still a virgin but I've done pretty much everything except have sex and I think I'll probably lose my virginity soon. I wanted to sleep with my ex but he went all weird on the idea and we broke up.'*

It's easy to get carried away or caught up in the moment and when you're turned on it's not always easy to stop. But even if you're ready for sex, you've still got to ask yourself one more question: are you ready to become a parent?

If you don't use contraception, then having sex could easily end up in a pregnancy. So before you get busy, get safe.

There are lots of myths about ways girls can stop themselves from getting pregnant ...

→ Girls can't get pregnant the first time they have sex. LIE
→ Girls can't get pregnant if they have sex standing up. LIE
→ Girls can't get pregnant during their period. LIE
→ Girls can't get pregnant if they take a bath after having sex. LIE
→ Girls can't get pregnant if they have a pee straight after having sex. LIE
→ Drinking vinegar before sex stops girls getting pregnant. LIE
→ Jumping up and down after sex stops girls getting pregnant. LIE
→ Girls can't get pregnant if they stand on a telephone directory during sex. LIE
→ Drinking alcohol before sex stops girls getting pregnant. LIE

If semen travels up a girl's vagina and meets one of her eggs the girl will get pregnant. The only way to stop a girl from getting pregnant is to prevent semen and eggs from coming into contact with one another.

### What's the best way to do that?

The only one hundred per cent effective way of preventing pregnancy is not to have sex. If you're not ready to take a vow of abstinence but you don't want to be a parent right now, you have to use contraception.

Contraceptives are things people use to stop women from getting pregnant – like condoms or the pill. Some religions and cultures (like Catholicism) don't allow the use of contraceptives, so people have to try and use other methods of birth control. Those methods are a bit risky ...

## THE RHYTHM METHOD OR 'NATURAL FAMILY PLANNING'

The rhythm method is based on the woman working out which days in the month she is fertile (most likely to fall pregnant). On those days she doesn't have sex.

### Does it work?

Hmm – it's risky! It's hard to calculate fertile days properly. These days there are different kits (like the fertility monitor Persona) that have been invented to help girls work out what's going on inside them. The girl has to make a note of her body temperature every day and look at the other changes in her body – like subtle changes in her vaginal discharge – to see when she's likely to conceive.

The problem is that lots of girls don't have totally regular menstrual cycles (the menstrual cycle is the process that happens in a girl's body every month: her ovaries release an egg, it travels down the Fallopian tubes to her uterus and then, if it doesn't meet a sperm, it gets washed away in her period). As the process isn't completely regular it's hard to work out exactly when the egg is in the Fallopian tubes (where it might meet a sperm). Another problem is that sperm can live for several days. If a girl has sex a few days before her most fertile period, the sperm may still be alive when the egg is released. Doh!

## Why do people use the rhythm method?

People usually use the rhythm method because they're not allowed to use other methods of contraception. Other people use the method because it's natural and doesn't involve any devices being put into their bodies.

# EARLY WITHDRAWAL OR *COITUS INTERRUPTUS*

Early withdrawal is when a boy pulls his penis out of a girl's vagina before ejaculating (releasing semen from his penis).

## Does it work?

Early withdrawal is risky. One problem is that – although he may have every intention of pulling out in time – when a boy's having sex it can take a *lot* of willpower for him to actually do that.

The other problem is that before boys ejaculate they usually leak some pre-ejaculation fluid. This can contain sperm. So even if the boy pulls out before he comes (ejaculates), his pre-ejaculation fluid may already have sent sperm shooting up into the girl's vagina ...

## Why do people use the early withdrawal method?

As with the rhythm method, people usually use the early withdrawal method because they're not allowed to use other forms of contraception or because they see it as a 'natural' solution. Some people use it because they want to have sex but don't have any contraception on them ...

### King Condom

| | | | |
|---|---|---|---|
| The other big problem for men and women who aren't allowed to use contraception is that they can't | use condoms to protect themselves against sexually transmitted infections. Remember – | while there are lots of methods of contraception, condoms are the only things that also protect against STIs. | That's why, whatever else you use, you should also use a condom when you have sex. |

# CONDOMS

There are male condoms and there are female condoms (Femidoms). They both work by creating a barrier that sperm can't penetrate.

## *FEMALE CONDOMS*

Female condoms are tubes made of thin plastic that have an opening at one end. This end is attached to a large ring that stays outside the vagina. The rest of the condom goes inside. When you're having sex you need to make sure that the penis is going inside the Femidom because sometimes female condoms slip and the penis ends up being inserted between the condom and the vaginal wall. If that happens, the Femidom isn't a heck of a lot of use. All the sperm just goes sneaking up inside the girl's body.

### When do you put a female condom on?
You can put a female condom on at any point before you have sex or before your genitals touch. It can be a bit slippery and sloppy (it's not the most sexy thing in the world) but it's still worth using. Once you've finished having sex you can take it out whenever you want and throw it away.

### Does it work?
When a female condom is used properly it's about 95% effective in preventing pregnancy. It also gives you protection against STIs. Warning! If you're using a lubricant (something to increase wetness and slipperiness during sex) and wearing a condom, make sure the lubricant is water-based. Oil-based lubricants – like baby oil or butter or Vaseline – can damage the rubber of some condoms and create holes. If your condom's got a hole in it, it's useless.

### Where do you get female condoms from?
You can get female condoms free from some family-planning or sexual-health centres – or you can buy them from chemists or supermarkets.

## MALE CONDOMS

A male condom is a tube-shaped piece of thin plastic or latex (latex is either made of rubber or an artificial rubber-like substance). They have an opening at one end into which the boy fits his penis. Then the rest of the condom is rolled down over the penis so it looks a bit like a second skin. When the boy ejaculates, his semen collects at the bottom of the condom instead of going inside the girl's vagina.

### When do you put a male condom on?

You put a male condom on as soon as the penis gets erect and before it goes near the vagina! Once a boy's ejaculated he should withdraw, holding on to the condom to stop any semen spilling out.

### Does it work?

When it's used properly a male condom is about 94–98% effective at preventing pregnancy. Remember that male condoms are thin so they can get rips and tears in them. If they are ripped in any way, they won't work. Plus, if you're using a lubricant (something to increase wetness and slipperiness during sex) and wearing a condom, make sure the lubricant is water-based. Oil-based lubricants – like baby oil or butter or Vaseline – can damage some condoms.

### What sort of male condom should I use?

There are loads of different condoms to choose from. The most important thing is to check that the condom packet is marked with the BSI Kitemark (BS EN 600) and/or the European CE mark. That means the condom's reached an approved standard – it's a quality condom! It's also important to check the expiry date marked on the packet. Out-of-date condoms are more likely to rip or tear.

Once you know the condom's safe you've still got some choices to make. Do you fancy a ...

→ **Black condom**
Black condoms are designed for people with dark skin tones.

→ **Coloured condom**
There's no reason why they're coloured – it's just for fun. It can be a bit weird staring down at a bright blue, fluorescent green or scary red willy though!

→ **Extra-strong condom**
These are tough condoms and the sort that are the least likely to break. If you're having anal sex (where the penis is inserted into the anus rather than the vagina) then these are the condoms you should use. The other type of condom that is recommended for anal sex is a condom designed specifically for gay men. These are distributed by an organisation called Freedom and they come in little black packets. They're given out for free by some gay support groups and in gay bars and clubs.

→ **Flavoured condom**
Flavoured condoms are meant to taste nice (but don't get carried away and try munching them). You can get chocolate-flavoured condoms, banana-flavoured condoms, curry-flavoured condoms (yeuch) ... Remember that flavoured condoms have been designed with oral sex in mind, so check on the packet before using them for penetrative sex – they may not be strong enough.

→ **Novelty condom**
Novelty condoms are condoms that come in weird shapes and designs – like bumps and bulges or animal heads or little faces. They're a laugh, but make sure they've been quality-approved (have the BSI Kitemark or European CE mark).

→ **Ribbed condom**
Ribbed condoms have tiny ridged hoops running down them. They're supposed to provide extra sensation for girls ...

→ **Spermicidally lubricated condom**
Spermicide is a substance that destroys sperm. These condoms are coated in spermicide and so provide extra protection against pregnancy.

→ **Non-spermicidally lubricated condom**
Some people are allergic to spermicide so non-spermicidally lubricated condoms have been designed for them.

→ **Testicle-cover condom**
  The name gives it away a bit – these condoms don't just cover a boy's penis, they cover his testicles too. That makes them even better protection against STIs than normal condoms because more of the genital area is protected.

→ **Ultrafine condom**
  Ultrafine condoms are very thin condoms that are meant to provide greater sensation (but they're also fragile so don't go ripping them by mistake).

→ **X-large condom**
  Some blokes have very large penises, and standard condoms can feel too tight for them. X-large condoms have been designed for these guys. But condoms are meant to be 'snug', so don't wear an X-large condom if it feels at all loose. If it's loose it's likely to slip off.

## Where can you get male condoms?

Male condoms are given away free at family-planning and sexual health clinics, you can buy them in places like chemists, supermarkets or garages, or you can buy them from slot machines in bars, clubs or pub toilets.

## DIAPHRAGMS

A diaphragm (or a cap, a smaller type of diaphragm) is a dome-shaped piece of soft rubber that's fitted over a girl's cervix. The cervix is the entrance to the womb.

Diaphragms act as barriers and prevent sperm from travelling up inside the girl.

### Do they work?

If it's fitted properly and spermicide is also used, a diaphragm is 92–96% effective at preventing pregnancy. (Spermicides are lotions – like foams or creams – that kill sperm. They need to be squirted inside the vagina before sex or squirted into the diaphragm before insertion.)

Diaphragms need to be inserted one to two hours before sex. They should stay in for six hours after sex and then they should be removed. Every time you have sex with the diaphragm in you should apply more spermicide.

It can be hard to get used to inserting a diaphragm correctly and you have to use spermicide to make it properly effective. So if you're allergic to spermicide, this isn't a good option for you.

If you're using a diaphragm as your birth-control method, look after it properly. Check regularly to make sure it doesn't have any rips in it and don't get any oil-based products – like baby oil or Vaseline – on it. These can damage rubber.

Diaphragms are only effective at preventing pregnancies. They don't offer protection against sexually transmitted infections. To be safe you should also use a condom.

### Where can you get diaphragms?
You have to be fitted for a diaphragm by a doctor. They'll let you know what size you need and how to insert it properly. You can either ask your GP or go to a family planning clinic.

Diaphragms are free when you get them from your doctor but, once you know your size, you can buy replacements from your chemist. But do go back and see your doctor or nurse every six to twelve months to check that the diaphragm still fits. If you put on or lose weight, you may need a different size.

## CONTRACEPTIVE IMPLANTS

At the moment there's only one type of contraceptive implant available in the UK. It's called Norplant. Norplant is made of six soft, matchstick-shaped tubes that are implanted into the upper arm and release hormones that prevent pregnancy.

### Does it work?
Norplant lasts for five years. For the first year it's 99% effective in preventing pregnancy and after that it becomes 98% effective.

It doesn't work if it's used at the same time as some medicines (like the ones used to treat epilepsy). You need to let the doctor know if you're taking any medicine before and during your time wearing the implant.

Implants don't protect against sexually transmitted infections, so to be safe you should also wear a condom.

**Where can you get implants?**
You need to go to a specially trained doctor or nurse to have an implant put in.

Implants aren't suitable for everyone and your doctor will be able to tell you whether or not they're right for you. You need a checkup three months after the implant is first fitted and then you need a checkup once a year.

## CONTRACEPTIVE INJECTIONS

A contraceptive injection is an injection of hormones that prevent pregnancy. Using a needle, the hormones are injected into a muscle in the body (normally a muscle in your bum).

There are two types of contraceptive injection. One's called Depo-Provera and it's effective for twelve weeks. The other one's called Noristerat and it's effective for eight weeks.

**Do they work?**
Contraceptive injections are 99% effective at preventing pregnancy but their effectiveness decreases if you don't have the injections done regularly or if you're taking medicine that interrupts the hormones. You need to let the doctor know if you're using any medicines before and while you're on the injections.

Again, contraceptive injections don't protect against STIs. Be safe and wear a condom.

### Where can you get contraceptive injections?
You need to go to a doctor to get a contraceptive injection. It's free but it's not suitable for everyone. Your doctor will be able to tell you if it's right for you or not.

## IUD

IUD stands for intrauterine device (they used to be called coils). They're made of plastic and copper and they fit inside a girl's womb and prevent sperm from getting to eggs. They also prevent eggs from settling inside the womb. Depending on which IUD is used, it can be left in the womb for between three and ten years.

### Do they work?
IUDs are 98–99% effective at preventing pregnancies. The downside is that some IUDs can make girls' periods more painful and there's a small chance they'll cause an infection. If you feel unwell or in pain or if you think the IUD might have slipped, go and check it out with the doctor.

You still need to use a condom when you're using an IUD because they do not offer any protection against sexually transmitted infections.

### Where do you get IUDs?

You need to go to a specially trained doctor or nurse to have an IUD fitted (ask your GP or in a family-planning or sexual-health clinic). It's free but they're not right for everyone – ask your doctor if it's a good option for you.

## IUS

IUS stands for intrauterine system (intrauterine basically just means inside the womb). It's made of plastic and it fits inside a girl's womb and releases hormones that stop her getting pregnant. An IUS can last for up to five years.

### Does it work?

An IUS is over 99% effective at preventing pregnancies. It starts working as soon as it's put in and – bonus – it can help to reduce period pain! Sometimes an IUS can get dislodged, so it's important to check it regularly (the doctor can show you how).

(And no, they don't offer protection against STIs. Make sure that condom's handy ...)

### Where do you get IUSs?

Your GP, family-planning or sexual-health clinic will be able to put you in touch with a specially trained doctor or nurse who'll get your IUS fitted. You can get an IUS for free, but talk to the doctor first to find out whether they're the best contraceptive method for you.

## THE PILL

Contraceptive pills are also known as oral contraception or as birth-control pills.

There are two main types:
→ **The combined pill**
→ **The progestogen-only pill**

### THE COMBINED PILL

There are lots of different brands of combined pill, and girls often have to try a few before they find the one that suits them best. But they all work in the same way. They stop eggs being released from the ovaries and they make it harder for sperm to travel through a girl's body. They're called combined pills because they contain a combination of two hormones – oestrogen and progestogen.

### Does the combined pill work?

If the combined pill is taken properly, it's 99% effective at preventing pregnancy. Different combined pills are taken in slightly different ways, so make sure you read the instructions on the packet. If you forget to take a pill or you're taking antibiotics – or you're sick and you throw the pill up – then it's not going to be as effective as it should be and you run the risk of getting pregnant. If you think you might have done something that will mess up its effectiveness, go and talk to the doctor and take extra precautions when you're having sex.

You should be using condoms at the same time as the pill anyway because the pill only protects against pregnancy. You need the condoms to protect yourself against sexually transmitted infections.

### Where do you get the combined pill?
You have to have the pill prescribed for you by a doctor.

### *THE PROGESTOGEN-ONLY PILL*

The progestogen-only pill is also known as the 'mini-pill' because it only contains one hormone ... progestogen! It works by thinning out the lining of the womb and making it unsuitable for a fertilised egg. The progestogen also makes the mucus (slimy secretion) in a girl's cervix get thicker and act as a barrier that the sperm can't penetrate (it's kind of like death by bogey for the sperm).

### Does it work?
If the mini-pill is taken correctly, it's 98% effective at preventing pregnancy. But you have to take it at the same time each day (to within three hours) or it won't work. You're also in trouble if you vomit or have diarrhoea, because that might wash the pill out of your system before it's had a chance to work. If this happens, you need to see the doctor and take extra precautions when you're having sex.

Remember – the mini-pill only protects against pregnancy. To protect yourself from STIs you also need to use a condom.

**Where can you get the mini-pill?**
Your doctor has to prescribe you the mini-pill.

# EMERGENCY CONTRACEPTIVE PILL

The emergency contraceptive pill is nicknamed the morning-after pill. It contains a very strong dose of hormones that either prevent a girl's ovaries from releasing an egg, or stop sperm from reaching the egg, or stop a fertilised egg from settling in the womb and starting to develop into a baby.

IT IS ONLY MEANT TO BE USED IN AN EMERGENCY.

Some people seem to think it's OK to have unprotected sex because they can just go and take emergency contraception. That's dumb. Taking emergency contraception is not as reliable as regularly using normal contraception. It can also make girls feel ill.

*But*, if you do have unprotected sex – maybe because you got carried away or your condom broke or you messed up with the pill – then you need to take the emergency contraceptive pill as soon as possible. For it to work it needs to be taken within 72 hours of the time when you had sex.

Emergency contraception is available from GPs, family-planning and sexual-health clinics, from some chemists and from some hospitals. You're given two pills. You take one immediately and one twelve hours later.

Some people react badly to the emergency contraceptive pill. It makes them feel ill and it can make them vomit. If you throw up within two hours of taking the first pill, take the second pill immediately, call the person who gave you the pill, explain what happened and ask for another one. If you throw up after the second pill, call the person who provided the pill and ask for advice.

**Does emergency contraception work?**
If you take the emergency contraceptive pill within 24 hours of having unprotected sex, it's 95% effective. If you take it within 25–48 hours, it's 85% effective.

# FOREPLAY

Any touching, kissing or oral sex that ends in penetrative sex is described as foreplay. People often have foreplay before sex because it's fun and because it relaxes the body and makes sex easier.

# PENETRATIVE SEX

Penetrative sex is what people usually mean when they talk about sex. It can either be vaginal sex – when the penis is inserted into the vagina – or anal sex, when the penis is inserted into the anus (bottom).

## VAGINAL SEX

In vaginal sex the penis is inserted into the vagina and moved around until the boy is so stimulated he comes (ejaculates). The more boys get used to sex, the better they get at stopping themselves from ejaculating – so hopefully they can hold on until the girl comes too!

*Sarah, 20, says: 'I'd always had this thing about wanting to be in love with the first person I slept with. I was really in love with my first boyfriend but I was fifteen when I went out with him and I didn't feel ready to go the whole way. And then he dumped me anyway. So, after that I went out with other people but I didn't feel like I loved them and I didn't want any of them to be my first. In the end I didn't have sex until I was nineteen – and I only had it then 'cos I was fed up with being a virgin. I wasn't that into the guy and it wasn't that great an experience. I wish I'd kept on waiting 'cos now I've met someone I really like ...'*

*Max, 17, says: 'I had sex for the first time when I was fourteen. I was going out with a sixteen-year-old – she thought I was fifteen! – and she initiated it. I wanted to do it but it was more about impressing my mates than anything else.'*

*Antony, 18, says: 'I was at a boys' school and I didn't really get to know any girls until I was sixteen. I started going out with a girl when I was seventeen – we were both virgins and for ages we just didn't bring up sex. I think we were both scared! Then we did talk about it and went through this phase of 'almost' doing it and then wussing out. And then when we did finally do it, it was all over pretty quickly (erm, yeah, my fault). But it's got a lot better since then.'*

*Louise, 16, says: 'I was scared that I wouldn't be any good at sex. I kept imagining that my boyfriend would think I was rubbish and dump me or that I would move wrong or make weird noises or something. I was too embarrassed to talk to him about it at first but all my friends said I had to tell him how I was feeling. So I did and after we talked I felt a lot more relaxed 'cos he said that he wasn't just with me for sex and if I wasn't ready he'd wait. It still took a few months before it happened but it was fine. And we're still together so I can't have been that bad!'*

People worry about having sex – especially the first time they do it. They might think they're going to do something wrong or not be able to perform or not be as good at sex as the other people their boyfriend/girlfriend has slept with. They might also worry that they're going to hurt the other person – or get hurt themselves – or that the other person is just using them.

All those worries are another reason why you should be very comfortable with another person before you have sex with them. You need to be able to tell them how you're feeling and to know that if you decide you're not ready to take the step of having sex, you can tell them to stop.

Remember – you're allowed to stop at any time. That might be frustrating for the other person, but they'll just have to deal with it. You have to want it too.

## COMMON WORRIES

→ **He's/She's just using me for sex**
   Some people are really immature about sex. They just want to do it as often as they can with as many people as they can and then brag about it with their mates. The problem is that if someone's using you for sex, but you're having sex with them because you genuinely care about them, you'll end up feeling used and hurt. The best way to avoid this situation is to make

sure you really know the other person before you have sex with them.

### → I won't know how to do it

No one knows exactly what they're doing the first time they have sex – but it's one of those things that people do instinctively. If you're comfortable and relaxed and you want to be having sex, then your body will respond to the other person's. Don't bother worrying about it – just go with it!

### → What if it hurts?

Girls worry about sex hurting them, and guys worry that they'll hurt the girl. First time sex does hurt sometimes – so you need to take things slowly.

• It can be painful for a girl if she's not 'wet' enough. When a boy gets turned on he gets an erection. When a girl gets turned on her vagina starts producing natural lubrication (slippery fluids) that make her wet and make it easier for the penis to move inside her. Girls' bodies can take longer to get aroused than boys', so spend as long as she needs on foreplay – don't jump into full-on sex straight away.

• If a girl is frightened by the thought of sex, her vaginal muscles can tighten up and make it impossible for the boy's penis to get inside her. Sometimes there's a physical reason for this and the girl will need to see her doctor, but more usually it happens because she isn't emotionally ready to go through with having sex. Don't try to force the issue, just stick to kissing and cuddling her until she's ready (and that doesn't mean later on that day!).

• Girls sometimes bleed the first time they have sex, because it breaks their hymen. The hymen is a thin piece of skin that covers the vagina. But often a girl is born without a hymen – or it's already been broken by the time she has sex. Hymens can get broken when people do sport or when they use tampons or when a girl gets fingered.

• If a boy has a huge penis, he can hurt a girl by thrusting too roughly. Boys who are well endowed need to make an extra effort to be gentle and not get too carried away.

### → What if I come too soon?

Most boys, at some time in their life, experience premature ejaculation. Premature ejaculation is when a boy comes –

orgasms and semen comes out of his penis – just before he starts to have sex or very soon after the sex has started. All the sexual excitement builds up and – boom – his penis takes on a life of its own.

There's no sure-fire way to stop premature ejaculation, but there are some tricks you can do to help.

• You can masturbate before you have sex. That should help calm you down for a while!

• When you go inside the girl you can move your hips round in a circle instead of thrusting in and out. That movement produces less sensation so it's easier to stay hard.

• Relax! If you worry about premature ejaculation, you can think yourself into doing it – so don't.

### → What if I lose my erection?

Sometimes erections just don't last. As if it's not bad enough having to cope with hard-ons that pop up when you don't want them around, you also have to cope with erections that wilt away when you do want them around! It's a pain but it happens to pretty much everyone. That's because – strange as this might seem – sometimes sex isn't the only thing on your mind. If you're feeling nervous or tense or tired or worried about something, those feelings can come barging in on you and send your erection crashing down.

If it happens – don't stress. Explain to the girl (or boy) you're with that it's nothing they've done that's made your erection vanish and that you've got stuff on your mind. If you reassure them it isn't something about them, they'll be understanding.

### → What if the girl doesn't come?

Girls can enjoy sex just as much as boys do, but it's not as easy for them to orgasm during vaginal sex as it is for boys. That's because the most sensitive area of their body – the clitoris – isn't really stimulated when the penis is inside the vagina. But in some positions boys can use their hands to stimulate the clitoris during sex. Don't put all the effort into achieving orgasm – just make sure you both enjoy yourselves.

### → What if the girl gets pregnant?

When a boy has sex with a girl there's always the risk that she will become pregnant. No form of contraception is one hundred per cent foolproof, but you've got a much better chance of avoiding pregnancy if you use birth control than if you don't …

# PREGNANCY

*Beth, 15, says: 'I'm fifteen years old and I've got a baby girl, Mandy, who's one. I got pregnant 'cos I was fooling around with my boyfriend and he wasn't wearing a condom. When I found out I was pregnant I didn't know what to do. My boyfriend didn't want the baby – he said he'd give me the money to have an abortion but I didn't feel like I could do that. So I kept her and Mum's helping me to look after her. My boyfriend's moved away. I have to get up at five-thirty in the morning to give her her bottle, I haven't got any qualifications and I can't get a job. I love Mandy but I wouldn't tell anyone else my age to have a baby – I'd say wait until you've finished growing up yourself.'*

*Clare, 18, says: 'I was on the pill so I didn't think there was any chance I'd get pregnant. But I got ill and the doctor put me on antibiotics and I think they stopped the pill working because I started putting on weight and I couldn't work out why. After a few months I went to the doctor and he said I was pregnant and it was too late to have an abortion. I didn't want a child this early – I wanted to go to university and become a vet. But now I've got to look after Elise.'*

*Jim, 16, says: 'When my girlfriend told me she was pregnant I couldn't speak. I couldn't even think. I was just scared. I was thinking about what her parents were going to do to me and what my mum would say. I didn't want a child – I wanted her to get rid of it. But then I started changing my mind and feeling like it was my responsibility and it was a proper little person and we should keep it. But in the end she decided we wouldn't be able to look after it and she had an abortion. We still haven't really talked about it. We broke up but I still see her around. It just feels weird talking about little things with her now – I'd prefer it if I didn't see her.'*

## Is it possible you're pregnant?

Oral and anal sex don't make girls pregnant, but any time a girl has vaginal sex with a boy she's running the risk of conceiving a child. If a couple do *anything* that let sperm get inside the vagina (maybe the girl gave the boy a hand job and then touched herself) they could end up facing the prospect of being parents ...

### How can you tell if you're pregnant?

If you think anything unusual is happening to your body and there's any chance you might be pregnant, do a pregnancy test or go and see your doctor. It seems weird but sometimes girls just don't realise they're pregnant. There've been stories in the newspapers about teenagers getting stomach pains – and a few hours later giving birth to a baby. All the time they'd been pregnant they'd still been having their period and they hadn't noticed that they were putting on weight.

Luckily, most girls do have symptoms of pregnancy. These include:

- → **Missing their periods.**
- → **Having periods that are much lighter than normal.**
- → **Having sore or tender breasts.**
- → **Feeling sick.**
- → **Feeling light-headed.**
- → **Feeling more tired than usual.**
- → **Peeing a lot.**
- → **Feeling like they're bloating or putting on weight.**
- → **Their appetite changes.**

Having one or more of these symptoms doesn't mean you are pregnant (for instance, if your period's late it doesn't necessarily mean you're pregnant, it could be a sign you're stressed or ill) but if you're at all worried, take a pregnancy test.

The doctor can give you a pregnancy test or you can buy a home pregnancy test at the chemist. They're easy to use and they come with full instructions. You have to hold a spatula-shaped stick under you while you pee and this detects whether or not a certain hormone is present in your body. If it is, you're pregnant and if it's not, you're not.

Home pregnancy tests are pretty accurate, but, if you've taken the test less than two weeks after having sex, there's a possibility that the hormone hasn't had a chance to show up in your body yet. If the test is negative but your period doesn't start on time, take another test.

## What should you do if you (or your girlfriend) are pregnant?

If the pregnancy test is positive, then you've got some big decisions to make. It's the girl who gets pregnant and it's her body that's affected, but whatever decision is made about the baby affects the boy too.

If you are able to discuss the situation and support one another, it will help you both, but ultimately the choice is down to the girl. Deciding what to do when you're pregnant is tough.

You have to make a choice between:

→ **Keeping the baby.**
→ **Having the baby and then putting it up for adoption.**
→ **Having an abortion (an operation to end your pregnancy).**

Before you make that choice you need to think about:

→ **How would your life change if you kept the baby?**
→ **Why would you want to keep the baby?**
→ **How would you find the money to look after a baby?**
→ **Would you have people who could support and help you while you looked after the baby?**
→ **How would you feel if you gave birth and then gave the baby away for adoption?**
→ **How would you feel if you had an abortion?**
→ **Why would you want to have an abortion?**
→ **How would you pay for the abortion?**

It's your decision. You might have very strong feelings about abortion that mean it's not an option for you, or you might feel like you're in a situation where your only choice is to have an abortion. If you're not sure what to do, think very carefully about your choices before coming to a decision.

Having a baby would change your life for ever.

*Sam, 15, says: 'I wouldn't know what to do if I got pregnant. I'd be too young to give the child a decent life but I don't know if I'd be able to go ahead with an abortion – especially if I was in love with the baby's father. But I don't think it would be easy to spend nine months being pregnant and then let the baby be adopted. I just don't know what I'd do.'*

## Keeping the baby

If you decide to keep the baby, then there are a lot of things you need to start thinking about:

→ **What's your relationship like with your boyfriend?**
Legally, the boy has to pay contributions towards the baby's upkeep, but do you or he want him to play a bigger part in the baby's life? If you do, what's it going to be and how are you going to manage it?

→ **How are you going to pay for everything your baby will need?**
You'll be entitled to some money from the government but you'll have to contact the social services department of your local council to find out how much you'll be given.

→ **Who's going to offer you help and support?**
Looking after a baby is exhausting. Are there people who will be able to help you?

→ **Are you healthy?**
It's dangerous to smoke, drink, take drugs or eat unhealthily when you're pregnant. Doing any of those things can damage your baby.

→ **Where are you going to live?**
Will you be able to stay at home or will you have to move out? Where will you go?

→ **Do you know what to expect when you give birth?**
You need to work out where you're going to have the baby – in hospital or at home. You also need to go to classes to learn about giving birth.

## ADOPTION

If you don't want to have an abortion but don't think you'd be able to cope with bringing up your baby, you could arrange to have it adopted. That means you'd be giving up all legal rights to parental responsibility – but, if you wanted to, you would probably still be able to see or communicate with your child.

Adoption would either be carried out by the social services department of your local council or through an adoption agency. Talk to your GP or to the social worker at your local hospital – they'll be able to contact the right people.

If you're married, then both parents need to give their consent before the baby can be adopted – if you aren't married then, legally, the only person who needs to give their consent is the girl. But it is better if both the boy and the girl can talk about what they want. You can also change your mind about giving away your baby right up until the time of the court hearing – and that won't be until after your baby's been born.

## ABORTION

When a girl has an abortion the fertilised egg, the foetus, is removed from her womb.

Abortion is illegal in Northern Ireland but it's legal in the rest of the UK. If a girl decides to have an abortion, she doesn't need permission from her parents or her boyfriend to do it but she does need to get permission from two different doctors. The doctors will want to know how long she's been pregnant and why she wants to have the abortion before they let her go ahead with it.

Girls can have abortions until they're 24 weeks pregnant. The earlier the abortion is carried out, the safer and easier it will be.

Properly carried out abortions aren't dangerous and won't stop you having a baby in the future, but it's *very* dangerous to try and abort a baby yourself.

### How are abortions carried out?

Abortions are carried out in hospitals or private clinics. The length of time people have to stay can vary from a few hours to a couple of days. This depends on how long they've been pregnant and whether or not they want to have an anaesthetic (something to stop you from feeling pain).

There are two different ways of carrying out an abortion. One involves taking a pill. The pill contains drugs that make your body have a miscarriage (where the foetus is dislodged from the womb). This method can be used on people who are less than nine weeks pregnant. The other method involves an operation in which the foetus is surgically removed from the womb. This can be done right up until someone is 24 weeks pregnant.

### How do people feel after an abortion?

Physically, you can feel a bit of pain and cramps in your stomach. This should go away fairly quickly, but if it seems to be dragging on, go and see a doctor. It's possible that you've caught an infection.

Emotionally, people can feel anything from relieved to depressed. If you want to, the hospital or clinic should be able to put you in touch with people you can talk to about the way you're feeling.

## ANAL SEX

Some heterosexual couples do try anal sex, but it's more commonly associated with sex between men. It's the word used to describe sex when the penis is inserted into the anus rather than the vagina. Unlike the vagina, the anus doesn't produce natural lubrication. Even if an artificial lubricant – a substance providing moisture – is used, anal sex is still likely to tear the skin, making it easier for sexually transmitted infections to pass between partners.

If you're having anal sex, you must use an extra-strong condom and a water-based lubricant. Oil-based lubricants (like butter or baby oil) can damage rubber condoms.

## anal sex and the law

| | | |
|---|---|---|
| • In England and Wales it's illegal to have anal sex when you're under sixteen. | • There are no laws about anal sex in Scotland. | • In Northern Ireland it's illegal to have anal sex no matter how old you are. |

# RAPE

*Eleanor, 19, says: 'Last year I was invited to my friend Justin's 21st birthday party. Actually he wasn't really a friend, he was someone I'd had a crush on for ages. He knew how I felt and we'd had this on-off thing going on but then I found out he was seeing someone else at the same time and telling everyone she was his girlfriend. I'd been really hurt and I just hadn't wanted to see him since. But then this invitation arrived and I thought it would be petty not to go along if he was trying to be friends.*

*On the night I was really nervous though, so I drank about half a bottle of wine just while I was getting dressed. Then when I got to the party I saw that Justin's girlfriend was there, which made me feel terrible. I grabbed another drink and these boys invited me for a smoke. They were passing round a joint and I took some – I just wanted to be out of it so I could deal with the way everything was making me feel.*

*I don't know what happened next. I must have passed out 'cos my eyes opened and it was dark and I was lying in the same bedroom where I'd been smoking with the boys. Only I was on the bed and one of the boys was on top of me, touching my breasts. Something weird had happened 'cos I couldn't move my body and I couldn't speak but I was awake and I knew my jeans were undone. The boy saw my eyes were open and he kept saying, "Ellie? Ellie?" and he slapped me around the face.*

*When I didn't move he started touching me again. And then, I don't know, I seemed to come back into my body and I was able to move. I pushed him and started screaming and then Justin came rushing in. The boy got off me and I flew off the bed and started screaming hysterically. Justin tried to calm me down but he couldn't. I didn't know what the boys had done to me or why I'd passed out, I was terrified and I just wanted to get out of there. I can remember running out on the street and being so scared that the boy was going to come out after me. I ran as fast as I could and then this police car stopped and a policeman got out. He asked me if I was OK. I didn't know what to do – I didn't know if I'd been raped or not and I was scared that if I said anything the boy would deny it or say that I'd been drunk and stoned and had agreed to have sex with him.*

*So I didn't tell the policeman what had happened. I just said that I was going home. I don't think he believed me because he drove me home and then asked me again if there was anything I'd like to report. I still said no.*

*A few days later one of Justin's friends – a girl – got in touch with me. She asked me if I was all right and if I knew what had happened. Apparently the boy who'd been on top of me when I woke up had been downstairs earlier asking people for a condom. She didn't know if anyone had given him one or not. She wanted to know if I was going to report it to the police and she told me she'd be a witness for me but I didn't want to go to the police, I didn't want to think about it. I didn't even go to the clinic to get myself checked out.*

*It still makes me feel sick to think about it. I don't know what happened to me that night – I just pretend to myself that all he did was touch me and that it didn't go any further ...'*

Being raped means being forced to have sex when you don't want to. It doesn't mean that you can only classify something as rape if you try to fight the attacker off – it's still rape if they do it to you and you're too scared to try and stop them or you're drunk or you're asleep. It happens to boys as well as to girls but only men can be accused of rape. That's because rape involves the penis entering the body.

But both women and men can be charged with indecent assault – touching someone in a sexual way who doesn't want to be touched – and both rape and indecent assault are serious crimes.

## rape and the law

• In England and Wales rape is defined as a man having vaginal or anal sex with someone against that person's will.
• In Scotland only non-consensual vaginal sex is considered rape. Anything else is defined as indecent assault.
• Male rape is not recognised by the law in Northern Ireland.

Being raped is a horrible experience. Unfortunately, a lot of rapes are committed by men who know their victims – either because they're friends or because they've been dating them. Whenever you go out with someone make sure another friend knows who you're with and where you're going.

But some rapists don't know their victims. Some people (boys and girls) get attacked because they're in the wrong place at the wrong time and they're on their own. You need to do everything you can to make sure that you don't put yourself in a risky situation:

→ Don't walk by yourself down dark or isolated streets.
→ Take public transport instead of walking home at night.
→ Phone home to let them know when to expect you.
→ Don't hitchhike.
→ Don't accept lifts from strangers.
→ Stay aware of what's going on around you.
→ Keep your keys in your hand so you can get into your house quickly.
→ Wear shoes and clothes that you can run in.
→ If you see someone acting suspiciously, walk into a shop or stay around other people until they've gone.
→ Carry a rape alarm.

If you are raped, don't ever think you're to blame or that you deserved to have that happen to you. You're not and you didn't. No one does.

If it does happen to you, there are some practical things that you can do that will help you and will help the police to stop the rapist hurting anyone else …

→ Tell someone what's happened as soon as you see someone. You might need that person to act as a witness for you and describe what sort of state you were in.

→ Go to the police immediately. Don't change your clothes and don't wash or shower. The police might need to do a physical examination of you and your clothes to get clues about the identity of your attacker.

→ **Contact a friend or a relative who can come with you to the police station or meet you there. You'll want to be with someone who can look after you.**

→ **Try and talk to someone about what happened to you. It's a good idea to contact an organisation that has people who've been trained to help victims of rape.**

## SEXUAL ABUSE

Sexual abuse is any sort of sexual act or situation that you are being forced into against your will. It could be being touched, kissed, raped – or it could be being forced to look at something you don't want to.

When this happens to people it can make them feel awful. They can get depressed, or feel dirty and ashamed and guilty. Some people feel suicidal or start hurting themselves in an attempt to deal with all the emotions.

Sadly, people are sexually abused by people they should be able to trust – like a family friend. This makes it even harder to report them. But whoever it is and whatever they're doing – if you don't like it you have to tell an adult you trust and let them help you. Don't let your abuser scare you into keeping quiet. This is a horrible situation to be in but you need to get help – if you don't tell anyone then no one will know you're in trouble. If you don't tell anyone the person who is abusing you might start doing this to someone else too, because they think they can get away with it.

You need to find someone you can talk to about all this. People who've been sexually abused can feel ashamed or feel that they're to blame for what happened. If you talk to other people who know what you've been through, it can help you to come to terms with it and to feel less alone.

## INCEST

Incest is the word to describe sex between two people who are related. It's illegal. If someone is doing something to you against your will, this is sexual abuse and you need to talk to an adult to make it stop. If you don't feel safe talking to someone at home or to a teacher, then you can ring an organisation like Childline and ask them for help and advice.

You should never feel like it's your fault if someone is doing this to you. You may have been told that it is your fault or that you will be punished if you tell anyone – this isn't true. If your abuser is trying to scare you into keeping quiet, they're doing it because they know that they are doing something wrong. Don't let them get away with it.

## PAEDOPHILES

Paedophiles are sex abusers who are attracted to children and young people. One place where paedophiles can easily get the opportunity to befriend the people they might want to attack is the Internet – just remember that when you're in a chat room, you don't really know if the people you're messaging are really who they say they are.

OK, so that can be difficult to remember when you're in the middle of a bit of online banter with someone. And paedophiles can be tricky to suss out.

But if you arrange to meet up with someone you've met online (even if they seem genuine or have sent you photos) be very careful. Meet in a public place, tell someone where you're going and if someone you're not expecting shows up – leave.

# SEXUALLY TRANSMITTED INFECTIONS

Feeling sexy is fun when you're comfortable with the person you're fooling around with, but before you go too far you should be clued-up about the things that can go wrong. One of the biggest problems with getting it on with someone is that you put yourself at risk of contracting a sexually transmitted infection ...

A sexually transmitted infection (STI) is an illness that can be caught when someone comes into contact with an infected person's bodily fluids (a bodily fluid is any liquid that is carried in the body – like blood or semen or saliva).

STIs can also be caught when someone who's infected lets their genitals touch another person's genitals.

STIs are also called:
→ **Sexually transmitted diseases (STDs)**
→ **Venereal diseases (VDs)**
→ **Genitourinary infections (GU infections)**

## How can you tell if you've caught an STI?

Some STIs don't have noticeable symptoms, so it can be impossible to tell if someone's infected. That's why it's so important to take care when you're doing anything sexual – and to have regular checkups.

Having said that, there are some warning signs to look out for:

→ **Blood in your urine.**
→ **Fluid coming out of your genitals that looks or smells unusual or nasty.**
→ **Pain when you have sex.**
→ **Pain when you pee.**
→ **Pain in the lower part of your stomach.**
→ **Redness or itchiness around your genitalia.**
→ **Lumps, spots, sores or blisters around your genitalia.**
→ **Feeling feverish.**
→ **Having swollen glands.**
→ **Experiencing weight loss or tiredness for no reason.**
→ **Having a sore throat that doesn't go away.**
→ **For girls, bleeding when it isn't your period.**

## How do you catch an STI?

Anyone who engages in sexual activity with another person is at risk of catching an STI. The most common way to catch one is to have penetrative sex with an infected person, but they can also be caught through oral sex (putting your mouth on someone's genitals) or letting your genitals rub against another person's. Drug-users can catch STIs if they share the needles they use to inject themselves, and sometimes babies are born with STIs because their mother was infected and gave it to them while they were in the womb.

## What can STIs do?

→ The sexually transmitted infection known as HIV/AIDS has no cure and can kill you.

→ STIs can cause pain in the pelvis, testicles, penis, joints and eyes.

→ Some STIs (like gonorrhoea or chlamydia) can leave you infertile or sterile (unable to have babies).

→ Some STIs (like genital warts) can lead to cervical cancer in women. The cervix is part of the womb – so men don't have one.

→ If you catch hepatitis B and you don't get it treated, in some cases it can lead to liver damage or even death.

→ If you catch syphilis and don't get it treated, it can lead to organ failure or even death.

## Can you stop yourself from catching an STI?

There are lots of things you can do to protect yourself against STIs. If you're a drug-user, never share injecting equipment and always make sure the needles you use are sterilised. If you're at risk through sex you need to:

→ Find out your partner's sexual history *before* you get down and get dirty.

→ If either you or your partner have had sex before, you should get checked for STIs by a health professional. Don't worry that anyone else would find out if you did this – the doctors have to keep your visit and the results of your test confidential (they're not allowed to tell anyone).

→ Go and get retested every time you change partners.

→ Always use condoms when you're having sex. Condoms are the best protection against STIs (unless you don't have sex at all, ever!). If you're giving a girl oral sex, then you can buy things called latex dams that cover the vagina and protect you against catching *anything*.

→ **If you see odd blisters or redness or anything that seems unusual on or around your partner's genitals, don't have sex and don't touch them. If there's a nasty smell, that could be a sign of an STI too. Ask them to go and get checked out.**

## What should I do if I think I've caught an STI?

Most STIs are easily cured but you need to get down to your local doctor, your nearest family-planning centre or your nearest sexual-health clinic right away. Sexual-health clinics are also called:

→ **Sexually-transmitted-disease (STD) clinics**
→ **Venereal-disease (VD) clinics**
→ **Genitourinary-medicine (GUM) clinics**
→ **Special clinics**
→ **Special treatment centres**

You can find them by looking them up in the phone book or by ringing one of the groups who help people with sexual-health issues – like the Family Planning Association or a Brook Advisory Centre. Don't be embarrassed – they deal with the same types of question all day.

If you go to your doctor or to a hospital, your visit is completely confidential. That means they're not allowed to tell anyone else about it unless you tell them they can. Your age doesn't matter – the same rules apply to everyone. If you go to a sexual-health clinic, you don't even have to tell them your name – you can make a name up.

The doctor will give you a checkup. They'll:

→ **Look at your genitals and your mouth.**
→ **They might take a blood sample.**
→ **They might take a urine sample.**
→ **They might take a sample of any discharge (fluid) that's coming out of your genitals.**

Once the results of the checkup come through (this can take a few days) they'll let you know if you have caught something. If the tests are negative (indicating that you haven't caught an STI) the doctors might advise you to come back for another test in six months' time. That's because some infections can be in your body for this long before they start to show up.

If you have caught an STI, the doctor will give you treatment to cure it (the only STI that isn't curable is HIV/AIDS).

They will also advise you to tell anyone you've been having sex with about the infection. This might be embarrassing, but it's really important to stop the infection from spreading. Plus your partner might be the person who gave you the infection. If they don't get treatment, they'll probably just infect you again.

If you really feel like you can't say anything to anyone, then talk to the doctor. In sexual-health clinics they might be able to send out contact slips to ask people to go and see their doctor or to go to a clinic. Don't worry – these contact slips won't mention your name.

REMEMBER: Doctors and nurses (including your GP) have to keep your visit confidential. They're not allowed to tell anyone about it.

*Fiona, 19, says: 'I'd been going out with my boyfriend for about three months when I cheated on him with a boy in one of my lectures. It was a drunken thing, we didn't use protection, and the next day all I wanted to do was forget about it. We ignored one another for a few weeks but then one day he came up to me and said he'd been diagnosed with chlamydia and I needed to go and get tested.*

*It was like a nightmare. I went to the clinic and the doctor told me the result would take a few days to come through. Then she asked me if I'd used a condom when I slept with this bloke. When I said I hadn't she said that meant there was a high chance I would have caught his chlamydia and I needed to make sure that anyone else I'd had sex with since knew the situation and got tested.*

*So I had to tell my boyfriend. I got dumped, which was fair enough, but it turned out we both had chlamydia. I don't know whether I caught it from my fling and gave it to my boyfriend or if my boyfriend gave it to me and I passed it on to the other boy. It's all been awful and the only good thing is that they found the chlamydia pretty quickly. Apparently it doesn't always show up and if it's not treated it can make you infertile. So I suppose in that way I've been lucky …'*

## CHLAMYDIA

Chlamydia is a bacterial infection that can be cured easily by taking antibiotics. The problem is that, just like lots of other STIs, people can be infected by chlamydia but not show any symptoms. That's why it's important to have sexual health checks and to wear condoms.

Signs of chlamydia can include:

→ **Pain during sex.**
→ **Pain when you pee.**
→ **Unusual-looking (or smelling) discharge.**
→ **Pain low down in the stomach.**
→ **Feeling fluey – a bit sick and hot.**

If chlamydia isn't treated it can lead to infertility.

## CRABS

Crabs is the word for little white lice that can get into your pubic hair and bite you. You don't need to have sex to catch these – you can get them from sharing clothes or blankets with someone or from touching an animal that's carrying them.

The doctor can give you a lotion to get rid of the pesky nippers, but you might need to use it several times – lice are tough to shake off. You'll have to wash any clothes or sheets or pets that might be crawling with them too.

Signs of crabs can include:

→ **You feel itchy.**
→ **You find little spots of blood in your underwear from where they've been biting you.**
→ **You spot them scurrying around in your pubes (pubic hair) – but you'd have to look closely.**

## GENITAL HERPES

*Susie, 17, says: 'I caught herpes from my boyfriend Mike. He had these spots on his penis and I used to squeeze them for him. I used to squeeze the ones on his face too! He didn't know what they were but he wasn't bothered by them so they didn't bother me either. But then I saw these blisters on my vagina and when I went to the doctor she told me I had herpes. Gross.'*

Genital herpes is a virus. Once you've caught it, it can be controlled by medicine but the virus stays in your body and can reappear. You're not infectious the whole time – you're only infectious when the virus is active. The first time you get herpes is normally when it's the most uncomfortable. People catch the virus if they come into contact with an active herpes sore.

Signs of herpes can include:

→ **Blisters on your genitals.**
→ **Itchiness.**
→ **Feeling achy, tired and hot.**
→ **Finding it hard to pee.**

If you've got active herpes sores anywhere on your body, try not to touch them. Wash your hands frequently and don't touch your face or your eyes – if the herpes virus gets into your eyes it can cause blindness.

If you're a girl and you become pregnant, you must tell the doctor that you've had herpes so that they can take care it doesn't affect the baby.

## GENITAL WARTS

Genital warts is a virus (its other name is Human Papilloma Virus). Doctors can get rid of warts by freezing them, burning them, lasering them or cutting them off. There are also medicines for dealing with them.

Signs of genital warts include:

→ **Seeing warts on your genitals! They can appear around the genitals, on the genitals or inside the genitals, be brown,** white or pink, and there can be a few of them or just one.

→ Itchiness.
If genital warts aren't treated they can keep right on growing.
In some cases they can lead to cervical cancer in women.

## GONORRHOEA

Gonorrhoea is a bacterial infection that's cured by taking antibiotics. It's also known as 'drip', 'clap' and 'sting'.

Signs of gonorrhoea include:

→ Pain when you pee.
→ Unusual looking or smelling discharge.
→ Sore or swollen genitals.
→ Sore throat.

If gonorrhoea isn't treated it can lead to infertility.

## HEPATITIS B

Hepatitis B is very infectious so it's easy to catch it if you come into contact with an infected person. It's carried in all the bodily fluids – including saliva – and that means you can catch it from kissing someone infected as well as through having oral or penetrative sex. You can even catch it from sharing an infected person's toothbrush.

Be very careful, because some people can have Hepatitis B but not show any symptoms.

Signs of Hepatitis B can include:

→ Rashes.
→ Your skin turning yellowish.
→ Achiness and tiredness.
→ Feeling sick.
→ Losing your appetite.

If Hepatitis B isn't treated, it can cause liver damage and even kill you.

## *HIV/AIDS*

HIV is a virus that is carried in the blood. Its full name is Human Immunodeficiency Virus. This virus breaks down the body's defensive systems and leaves it incapable of fighting off illnesses. Gradually HIV develops into AIDS, Acquired Immune Deficiency Syndrome. By this stage the immune (defence) system is badly damaged and if the infected person catches an illness they can't fight it off. That means they die from it. But people can have HIV for a long time – even for years – before their body starts to show the damage. Some people can go for years without realising they've been infected.

HIV is carried in blood, breast milk, semen and vaginal fluid. It is *not* found in vomit, sweat, tears, mucus (bogeys) or saliva.

People catch HIV through having penetrative sex with an infected person or through having oral sex with an infected person. It can be caught through oral sex if the person has cuts in their mouth and infected semen or vaginal juices pass through those cuts and enter the bloodstream. Wearing a condom can help to protect people but there is always a risk that a condom will split or tear.

People can also catch HIV if they're drug-users and they share their injecting equipment with an infected person. Mothers with HIV can pass the virus on to their babies while they're in the womb or through breast-feeding.

There are lots of myths about how people contract HIV. It *can't* be caught from a toilet seat or from sharing a swimming pool or from being bitten by a mosquito. Blood or semen or breast milk or vaginal juices have to pass directly from one person into another for infection to occur.

Signs of HIV include:

→ **Sore throat.**
→ **Feeling fluey, tired, hot and achy.**
→ **Having a red and blotchy rash on your body.**
→ **Having severe headaches.**

→ Having night sweats.
→ Having an aversion to light.
→ Diarrhoea.
→ Ulcers.
→ Swollen glands.
→ Weight loss.
→ Pain in your stomach.
→ Loss of appetite.

HIV can be caught by anyone – men or women, gay or straight. There is no cure.

## SYPHILIS

Syphilis is a bacterial infection that can be cured by antibiotics. It can be caught through sex, and if syphilitic sores appear in someone's mouth, it's possible to catch it by kissing them.

Signs of syphilis can include:

- Sores (at first these are wet and oozy and then they dry up).
- A rash, high temperature and headaches.

If syphilis isn't treated it can cause organ failure and in extreme cases people can die.

Make sure you know how to protect yourself against STIs before you get too into touching your boy/girl. Some STIs are spread through skin contact ...

# SEX DICTIONARY

**Abortion:** An operation to end pregnancy.

**Age of consent:** The age at which a girl is considered old enough to agree to sex; 16 in England Scotland and Wales, 17 in Northern Ireland.

**AIDS:** A sexually transmitted infection for which there is no cure.

**Anal intercourse:** Sex where the penis is inserted into the bottom.

**Aroused:** Sexually excited.

**Balls:** Testicles.

**Bent:** Homosexual.

**Bestiality:** Having sex with an animal.

**Bi:** Bisexual.

**Birth control:** Protection against pregnancy.

**Bisexual:** Feeling strong attraction towards men and women.

**Blow job:** Fellatio.

**Blue balls:** Achiness in a boy's testicles when he's sexually aroused.

**Blue movie:** A pornographic film.

**Bollocks:** Testicles.

**Boner:** Erection.

**Boning:** Having sex.

**Bonking:** Having sex.

**Boobs:** Breasts.

**Breasts:** Soft mounds of fat on a woman's chest. After pregnancy they produce milk to feed the baby.

**Buggery:** Anal intercourse.

**Bun in the oven:** Pregnant.

**Bush:** Pubic hair.

**Celibate:** Someone who chooses not to have sex.

**Circumcision:** When the foreskin is removed from a penis.

**Climax:** The peak of sexual feeling.

**Clit:** Clitoris.

**Clitoris:** A very sensitive part of the female genitalia.

**Cock:** Penis.

**Coitus:** Vaginal sex.

**Come:** Semen.

**Coming:** Ejaculating for the boy – having an orgasm for the girl.

**Coming out:** Telling other people you're homosexual.

**Condom:** A form of contraception that goes over the penis or vagina and stops sperm from entering the female body.

**Contraception:** Methods of preventing pregnancy.

**Copulation:** Sex.

**Cross-dressing:** Wearing clothes that are designed for the opposite sex.

**Crush:** An infatuation with someone.

**Cum:** Semen.

**Cunnilingus:** Performing oral sex on a woman.

**Cystitis:** A painful inflammation that makes you feel like you need to pee but also makes peeing painful.

**Dick:** Penis.

**Dildo:** A sex toy that's shaped like a penis and can be inserted into the body.

**Dirty thought:** A fantasy about a person or a situation that involves sexual activity.

**Doggy-style:** When the girl is bent over on her knees and the boy enters her from behind.

**Double Dutch method:** When you use double protection – the pill and a condom.

**Double standard:** The way that girls and boys are judged differently for doing the same thing. It's often used to describe the way that when a boy sleeps around he's seen as having achieved something and if a girl sleeps around she's considered dirty.

**Dry humping:** Simulating sex when you've got your clothes on.

**Ejaculation:** When semen comes out of the penis.

**Emergency contraception:** Contraception you can take if you have unprotected sex.

**Erection:** When a penis fills with blood and rises upwards.

**Erogenous zones:** Sensitive areas of the body that can make people feel turned on when touched.

**Erotica:** Kind of classy

pornography (see Pornography). Any sex scenes included in fine art or literature are called erotica.

**Eyeing up:** When you look someone up and down because you think they're sexy.

**Faking an orgasm:** When a woman pretends she's come.

**Fanny:** Vagina.

**Fanny farts:** The farting noise that's sometimes made when a penis is pulled out of the vagina.

**Fantasising:** Imagining things happening that make you feel turned on.

**Feeling up:** Touching another person's body.

**Fellatio:** Performing oral sex on a man.

**Female ejaculation:** When fluids come out of a woman's body when she orgasms.

**Fetish:** Something (not necessarily something sexual) that turns someone on.

**Fingering:** Putting fingers into a girl's vagina to masturbate her.

**Flasher:** Someone who exposes their body in public.

**Foreplay:** Kissing, cuddling and touching as a lead-up to sex.

**Foreskin:** The sleeve of skin that covers the penis.

**French letter:** Condom.

**Frigid:** Being sexually unresponsive.

**G-spot:** An erogenous zone inside the vagina. A lot of women don't know where theirs is – but when they find it, it's a great surprise!

**Gay:** Homosexual.

**Genital mutilation:** Cutting or damaging the genitals.

**Genitals:** The external sexual organs.

**Getting jiggy:** Having sex.

**Giving head:** Fellatio.

**Groping:** Touching and squeezing someone's body.

**Hard-on:** Erection.

**Head:** Tip of the penis.

**Heterosexual:** Being attracted to people of the opposite sex.

**Hickey:** Lovebite.

**HIV:** A sexually transmitted infection that develops into AIDS.

**Hole:** Vagina.

**Homophobia:** Hating or being scared of homosexuality.

**Homosexual:** Someone who is attracted to people of the same sex.

**Horn:** Erection.

**Horny:** Aroused.

**Hymen:** Thin piece of skin covering the vagina.

**Impotent:** Unable to have or sustain an erection.

**In the closet:** Phrase describing people who haven't told anyone they're gay.

**Incest:** Sexual activity between people who are closely related.

**Indecent assault:** Touching someone in a very sexual way without their permission. This is illegal.

**Intercourse:** Sex.

**Jacking off:** Masturbating.

**Jerking off:** Masturbating.

**Jism:** Semen.

**Jizz:** Semen.

**Johnny:** Condom.

**Juice:** Semen.

**Knob:** Penis.

**Knockers:** Breasts.

**KY Jelly:** A type of lubrication.

**Lezzer:** Lesbian.

**Load:** Semen.

**Lovebite:** Sucking someone's skin until it bruises and leaves a mark (this is often round and reddish).

**Lubrication:** A substance that adds moisture and slipperiness.

**Lust:** A strong desire for something or someone.

**Masochism:** Getting sexual pleasure from being hurt or humiliated.

**Masturbation:** Stimulating the external sexual organs.

**Melons:** Breasts.

**_Ménage à trois_:** When three people have sex together.

**Monogamy:** Having a sexual relationship with one person at a time.

**Morning-after pill:** Emergency contraception.

**Multiple orgasm:** Reaching the peak of sexual pleasure, then experiencing it again a short time later.

**'Nads:** Testicles.

**Nuts:** Testicles.

**Nymphomaniac:** A woman who feels a compulsion to have sex with lots of men but doesn't have lasting relationships with them.

**Oestrogen:** A female hormone.

**Oral sex:** Sex where the mouth comes into contact with the genitals.

**Orgasm:** The peak of sexual excitement.

**Orgy:** Having sex with a group of people.

**Paedophile:** A person who is sexually attracted to children.

**Penetration:** Inserting the penis into someone's body.

**Penis:** The male sexual organ.

**Petting:** Sexual activity – but not actual sex.

**Poof:** Homosexual.

**Popping the cherry:** Losing your virginity.

**Pornography:** Sex scenes in books or in pictures or on TV and films that are designed to make people sexually excited.

**Pregnant:** When a girl has a baby developing inside her.

**Premature ejaculation:** When a boy comes just before sex – or very soon after sex starts.

**Prostitute:** Someone who has sex in return for money.

**Puberty:** The maturing process when a child becomes an adult.

**Pubes:** Pubic hair.

**Pussy:** Vagina.

**Queen:** Homosexual.

**Queer:** Homosexual.

**Rape:** When someone forces another person to have sex against their will.

**Rubber:** Condom.

**Sadism:** Getting sexual pleasure from hurting someone else.

**Safe sex:** Protecting yourself against sexually transmitted infections.

**Screwing:** Having sex.

**Scrotum:** The pouch of skin containing the testicles.

**Semen:** Whitish fluid containing male sex cells, which will, if combined with a female egg, produce a baby. Comes out of the penis during sexual activity.

**Sexual harassment:** Unwelcome sexual comments or actions.

**Shaft:** The length of the penis.

**Shagging:** Having sex.

**Sheath:** Condom.

**Shooting your load:** Ejaculating.

**Sixty-nine:** A sexual position in which two people simultaneously give each other oral sex.

**Slag:** Slang for a girl who sleeps around.

**Slapper:** Slang for a girl who sleeps around.

**Slut:** Slang for a girl who sleeps around.

**Snogging:** Kissing.

**Sodomy:** Anal intercourse.

**Spanking the monkey:** Masturbating.

**Sperm:** Semen.

**Spunk:** Semen.

**Stalking:** Following someone and spying on their movements.

**Stiffy:** Erection.

**Straight:** Heterosexual.

**Stripping:** Taking your clothes off.

**Stud:** Slang for a man who's had sex with lots of girls. Complimentary.

**Tackle:** Penis.

**Testes:** Testicles.

**Testicles:** The male reproductive glands (where sperm are made).

**Testosterone:** A male sex hormone.

**Todger:** Penis.

**Tool:** Penis.

**Tossing off:** Masturbating.

**Transsexual:** Someone who feels like they've been born the wrong sex.

**Transvestite:** Someone who dresses up in clothes usually worn by the opposite sex.

**Trouser snake:** Penis.

**Turned on:** Aroused.

**Up the duff:** Pregnant.

**Vagina:** The opening in a girl's genitals.

**Vibrator:** A sex toy that vibrates – moves around.

**Virgin:** Someone who hasn't had sex. =ben

**Vulva:** The external female genitals.

**Wanking:** Masturbating.

**Wet dreams:** When a boy ejaculates during his sleep.

**Whore:** Prostitute.

**Willy:** Penis.

**Woody:** Erection.

# 3 YOUR MIND

Being a teenager can be a weird experience. As well as all the changes happening in your body you've got to cope with a whole load of new stresses. You want more freedom to live your own life and hang out with your mates but you've still got to live at home and rely on other people to pay the bills. Then you've got to worry about things like working out your sexuality, getting through important exams and finding out exactly who you are. It's not easy – and it's made even more complicated by the fact that when you're a teenager your body is producing hormones that can turn your emotions upside down.

People often experience feelings of intense loneliness or unhappiness or anger when they're teenagers. Sometimes they can feel all those things without even knowing where the feelings are coming from.

If that happens to you, it's horrible. And it's even harder if other things in your life start going wrong – in fact, it can be devastating. Sometimes people end up feeling depressed or even suicidal. If you ever feel like this, the best thing you can do is talk to someone about what you're going through. That might be a parent or a teacher or someone from a helpline. Talking about it will make you feel less alone – and it will give you a chance to work out exactly what is going wrong and what you can do about it.

## SELF-ESTEEM

One of the things that a lot of teenagers go through is feeling like they don't like themselves and that other people don't like them either. OK, so the truth is that some people you meet probably won't like you – or they'll think you're all right but they won't be that bothered about getting to know you. But if you let them, a lot of other people *will* like you – and some of them will become really close mates.

So, question number one – do you like yourself? Question number two – do you know why other people like you? If you've answered no to either (or both) of those questions, then you're in a self-esteem slump. Some people are good actors and seem to be able to hide the fact that they feel bad about themselves. If this is you, stop a minute. Is hiding the way you feel helping you – or is it making things harder for you? If it's making you feel like no one knows the real you – and they wouldn't like it if you let them know it – what you're doing is damaging yourself. One of the most important things that you can do when you're a teenager is work out how to express yourself honestly. It's when you show your true character to people that you make real friends and that you really feel fulfilled. That means letting them know your flaws and your insecurities as well as all your good bits. And no, that's not easy to do, but if you do it then you'll find that people start to trust you with all the things that they worry about. Then you'll all realise that everyone has hang-ups – and you can really support one another. If there's one person who you do really like or think is trustworthy, then try opening up to them a bit – without playing a part.

Other people get self-esteem slumps and they lose all their confidence – to the point where they can't even pretend they're feeling good about themselves. The problem is if you don't like yourself, it's a lot harder to relax around other people. If you're not relaxed you feel awkward, and that sends out awkward vibes to the people around you. So how do you solve that Catch-22 situation?

The first thing to remember is that no one is naturally confident. Even the most outgoing, friendly person can feel totally terrified that other people aren't going to like them. But what those people have worked out is that everyone else feels exactly the same way. So, instead of hanging back and hoping that someone will talk to them, they realise that someone's got to be the one to break the ice and they go and do it. People like them because they're the ones who make an effort to overcome their fear. So take a deep breath, smile and launch yourself into some small talk. It doesn't matter what you talk about – last night's TV or a recent film usually work ...

*Melissa, 15, says: 'I went to this party a few months ago and my friend's cousin was there. He was standing on his own not talking to anyone so I went up and started chatting. He was really hard work at first 'cos he wouldn't say much back but I kept going 'cos he doesn't live in our area and I knew he didn't really know anyone. He did eventually start talking properly and we ended up getting on really well. We kept in touch and recently he asked me out!'*

The other self-esteem thing to remember is you need to be yourself. If you try to pretend you're something you're not, you'll feel uncomfortable – and other people will realise you're faking it. It doesn't matter who you are – if you're genuine, the people who are like you will be drawn to you. That's the way it works. So if you're not Little Miss Clubber or Little Mr Sporty, don't worry about it. You wouldn't be happy hanging round clubs or discussing last night's game anyway. Talk about the things that you're interested in and passionate about and people will want to hear what you have to say. Honestly.

Still not convinced? Here are some tricks that might pep up your self-esteem and give you the confidence you need to start believing in yourself ...

→ **Hold your head high**
You know how people always say that first impressions are important? Well, people form first impressions of someone before they even open their mouth and speak to them. That's why if you shuffle into a room, hanging your head and not making eye contact, people are going to expect you to be terminally shy and avoid you. You need to practise walking into a room, holding your head up and walking tall, looking people in the eye and smiling. OK, so you might not feel like doing any of that, but it's guaranteed to make you feel more in control and happier with yourself if you do.

→ **Think positive**
If you dread something and expect it to turn out badly, then it's far more likely to go wrong. But if you think about all the positive things that could happen, you're setting yourself up for success. Plus, people like being around positive people. It makes them feel happier and like they've got more energy. So look on the bright side and think positive.

→ **Get the look**
Even if you're not feeling confident inside, if you're wearing clothes that make you feel good, your confidence will get a boost. So if you're in need of some extra va-va-voom, grab your favourite clothes out of the wardrobe, give them an iron and go strut your stuff!

→ **Go get 'em!**
People like people who are prepared to throw themselves into things and really go for it. So if there's something you want to try – acting, hang-gliding, bog-snorkelling – go for it. For one, you'll get to meet loads of new people who might turn into good mates and for two, it'll give you something interesting to talk about. So what if other people don't know why you're into it – you're the one living your life, not them.

Self-esteem doesn't come overnight. But everyone has got things about them that other people find interesting and attractive. Don't worry about what other people think – concentrate on working out what you like about yourself. When you do that everything else will start to fall into place.

# BULLYING

OK, so sometimes it's not easy to ignore other people – especially if they're bullying you and making your life miserable. And bullying happens to loads of people ...

*Sarah, 17, says: 'I was embarrassed about telling anyone that I was being bullied. Mum always acted like I should be the most popular girl in school 'cos I'm slim and I've got blonde hair. She always used to say things like, "You're the sort all the boys will like and all the girls will want to be like," but it wasn't like that at all. There was this group of girls who hated me. They used to come up behind me in the corridor and start talking about me in really loud voices saying I was up myself and thought I was too good for everyone else. Then they started spreading rumours about me, saying that I slept around and reckoned I could get anyone I wanted to. My friends told me to ignore it but it just got worse and worse and then one time they waited for me after school and beat me up. One girl punched me in the lip and it swelled up and started bleeding everywhere. When I got home I was crying and I ended up telling Mum everything. She wanted to go to the school but I was scared that if the girls were punished they'd just get worse. Instead I asked Mum if I could change school and as soon as I finished my GCSEs that was what I did.'*

*James, 14, says: 'I was bullied when I first got to secondary school. There was this group of lads who used to bump into me and make comments about the way I looked and nick my bag and throw it around. I was always getting in trouble with the teachers 'cos they'd steal my books and I'd have to say I'd lost them. But then one time I lost it with one of them and we ended up having a fight. I lost but I hurt him. They backed off after that.'*

People bully other people because it makes them feel better. Sometimes they pick on someone because it makes them feel like part of the group and the bullied person can be made to feel like an outsider. Sometimes they pick on them because they're insecure and being nasty to someone else gives them a feeling of power. And sometimes people bully people just because they're different from them – they've got different interests or accents or clothes. Whatever the reason it can be really upsetting.

But don't ever feel like you're causing it or that you must be a rubbish person because it's happening to you; if you're bullied, it's not a reflection on you – it's a reflection on the people who are doing it.

*Holly, 14, says: 'My sister was getting bullied at school and I hadn't known about it. This new girl had come into her class and had taken away her best friend and the two of them had started making fun of my sister. I couldn't work out why my sister had changed. She'd always been really lively and fun but she went all quiet and shy. And then one day I saw her coming out of the bath and she had these cuts up her arm. She'd been so unhappy she'd started cutting herself. When she told me what had been happening I was so angry. I went and talked to the girls and warned them to leave her alone. Since then they've been nicer to my sister and my sister's become good friends with some other girls in her class. But she's still different to the way she used to be.'*

It's hard not to be affected by bullies. They make people feel intimidated, isolated and unhappy. If you're being bullied then let someone – like your parents and your form teacher – know. This might sound like bad advice, because you may just feel like it would make the bullying worse, but telling the teachers is the only way to make it stop. If you're worried, do it at a time when you know the bullies won't know what you're doing. If you're worried they might come after you when you've left school, then always walk with someone – or if you're on the bus, stay downstairs near the driver. And be careful who you give your mobile number to – text-bullying is becoming more and more common and can be just as upsetting as other forms of bullying. If the bullies are making you feel so bad that you want to take time off school or you're hurting yourself, then you really, *really* must speak to someone – please. They're affecting your work, your future and your happiness. Don't let them win. If you really feel like you can't talk to anyone at school or at home, then you could e-mail or phone people who work somewhere like the Anti-Bullying campaign or Kidscape and ask for their advice. (See the 'Further Help' section at the end of the book for details.)

# ANXIETY

Anxiety is a nasty emotion. It's feeling afraid and tense and helpless. Everyone feels anxious now and again, especially when there's something stressful going on (like an important exam approaching), but sometimes anxiety starts to take over people's lives ...

*Karen, 16, says: 'My mum's agoraphobic – she gets terrified when she has to leave the house. She says she panics when she's in a crowd or somewhere she doesn't know and she starts feeling like she can't breathe or she's going to faint. It's really sad 'cos she doesn't really see many people – not unless they bother to come round and see her.'*

Having a phobia is basically being really afraid of something. People can have phobias about pretty much anything – from insects to strangers to seeing blood (even if they see the blood on a TV show). The amount a phobia affects someone's life depends on what they've got the phobia about. If someone gets terrified at the idea of speaking in public, their phobia is going to be a lot harder to deal with than a phobia about mountains (erm, unless the person with the phobia lives underneath Ben Nevis).

If you've got a phobia of something specific – like being afraid of snakes or of water – then it's a good idea to ask your doctor to recommend a therapist in your area. They're trained to help people overcome their fears. Therapy can also help if you've got a phobia about being in a particular social situation – like answering questions in class or talking to people during break. But you can also help yourself ...

→ **When you feel yourself getting anxious, try to overcome your anxiety rather than withdrawing from the situation.**

→ **Do your best to look people in the eye when you're talking to them.**

→ **Before you get into a social situation think about things you could talk about.**

→ **An easy way of starting a conversation is to ask questions – that way you're joining in but the other person has to do most of the talking!**

→ **Speak clearly. If you mumble, people won't hear you and you'll have to say it all over again.**

→ **Don't worry if there's a silence. There always are silences while people think up new things to say.**

→ **Don't be afraid of criticism. People have different opinions and that's what makes conversations interesting. Listen to what other people have to say but don't be afraid to make your own mind up.**

Phobias aren't the only way people have of expressing their anxiety. Some people suffer from a condition called generalised anxiety disorder where they worry for a long time (at least six months) about things that don't seem that scary or troubling. They feel scared about the future and they're constantly looking out for stuff that might go wrong. Along with all that worry they might also start:

→ **Feeling restless and on edge.**
→ **Having trouble sleeping.**
→ **Finding it hard to concentrate.**

→ **Getting tense.**
→ **Getting irritable.**

People who feel like this do need to go and talk to a health professional, because different people need to be treated in different ways. Some might be able to deal with their anxiety just through talking about it but others might need medication to help them cope with the way they're feeling.

Another form of anxiety is when people get panic attacks. These are scary because they seem to come out of the blue. People might start sweating or going red or feeling like their hearts are beating too fast. They might get pains in their chest and start feeling dizzy and weak. Sometimes they think they're having a heart attack and that makes them panic even more. But there is medication to help control panic attacks so if you think you're getting stressed and getting these, go and talk to your doctor.

*David, 18, says: 'I've had obsessive-compulsive disorder since I was about nine. I started developing these little routines and if they went wrong I had to stop what I was doing and start all over again. I always had to get out of bed on the same side and take a certain number of steps to get to the door. Then I had a special way of brushing my teeth. I had to go in a circular motion thirty times on the bottom left, thirty times bottom right, thirty times top left, thirty times top right. I had rituals for everything and it took ages to get anything done. To be honest, it still does.'*

Obsessive-compulsive disorder is another way of expressing anxiety. People who have it obsess about things they think they've done or think they might do or just over ideas that they don't seem able to get out of their heads. They also do things compulsively – they might feel the need to count things or check them or wash all the time. This can make it very hard for people with obsessive-compulsive disorder to get on with their lives – and they do need to talk to their doctor to try and work out what's causing them to behave like this.

# DEPRESSION

*Marlon, 18, says: 'I was depressed on and off all the way through school. I didn't know what was causing it – I just seemed to have this feeling all the time that I wasn't worth anything. I thought I looked wrong and said the wrong things and wore the wrong things and that no one understood me or wanted to get to know me because I wasn't a good enough person. Then I had to go away on this school trip and I felt totally out of it. When we got on the bus I didn't have anyone to sit with and I barely spoke to anyone that whole week. By the time I got back I felt like I didn't know how to speak to people. My parents didn't know what was wrong with me. They thought I was ill because I was lying in bed and didn't even have the energy to get up. But I wasn't sleeping. I couldn't sleep. I just lay in bed hating myself and my life and not being able to imagine a time when it could get any better. My parents eventually got me to the doctor and he diagnosed me with depression. He prescribed me some pills and sent me to counselling. It took a long time but things have got better now ...'*

Depression is horrible. It's feelings of unhappiness, anxiety, tiredness, moodiness ... not much fun, huh? Sometimes people get depressed and they know what's causing it. They might be worried about things or there might be something bad going on in their life. Or they might feel depressed because they don't like the way they look or their friends are treating them badly. But people can also get feelings of depression that seem to come out of nowhere and leave them feeling totally down. That's because sometimes depression is caused and/or intensified by chemical changes in the brain, and they don't have any control over it.

The good news is that there are things that help to get rid of depression. The first thing to do is to realise when you're getting depressed. If you know what's going on then it's less scary when you start feeling all those negative emotions. People express their feelings differently, so take a look at the list below and see if any of these things are things that you do:

→ **Feeling like there's no point in being alive.**

→ **Having bad arguments with your family or your friends – because you're feeling unhappy.**
→ **Getting tense and worried about stuff.**
→ **Wanting to hide away in your own room all the time.**
→ **Having lots of trouble sleeping.**
→ **Feeling tired all the time.**
→ **Not eating enough or eating too much.**
→ **Feeling like other people don't like you.**
→ **Telling lies or getting into trouble a lot.**

If you do feel like any of these things are like you, it doesn't necessarily mean that you're depressed. But you're probably unhappy and unhappiness leads to depression. So, if you know you're unhappy, it's a good idea to work out why you're feeling that way. Once you've worked out what's causing you to feel down you can start to work out what to do about it. If you're experiencing a kind of general feeling of being upset, then it's harder to deal with – but it's still possible. Whatever's causing your low, the best thing to do is to talk to someone. Once you talk about a feeling or a problem, it starts to seem easier to deal with – especially if you talk to someone who understands how you're feeling. Sometimes it's easy to talk to your friends or your family, but sometimes it's easier to talk to a counsellor, or to someone from an organisation like Childline, who'll know exactly where you're coming from.

The other thing to do when you know you're feeling depressed is to look after yourself. Do things you like doing – play music or read or paint. Accept that you might feel down for a while but that feelings change. You will start to feel better.

If you really do seem to be sunk in an unending feeling of depression, go and talk to a doctor. They'll understand how you're feeling – they see a lot of people with depression and, if they think you need it, they'll also be able to give you some helpful medication.

Another form of depression that some people are affected by is called manic-depressive illness. This is where people swing between totally different moods. For as long as three months someone might seem happy and hyper and energetic and really full of themselves; then suddenly their high will go and they'll become depressed, lacking in energy, tearful and achy. If you know someone who's like this, then they need to go and see a doctor to get themselves sorted out.

# SELF-HARM

Self-harm or self-mutilation is when someone deliberately hurts themselves ...

*Tracy, 19, says: 'I started to self-harm when I was thirteen. My parents had divorced and I'd had to move area and go to a new school where I didn't have any good friends. My sister had behavioural problems and my mum was having a hard time coping with her on her own. I used to feel awful because it made it worse for my sister that I could go out and she couldn't. And I felt guilty because I secretly wished I could go and live with my dad and go back to my old school instead of staying with my mum and my sister. I was really angry and confused and one night me and Mum had a fight. I ended up being so unhappy I was hysterical and I shut myself in my room and started hitting myself with a shoe. I wanted it to hurt so much it would make me concentrate on that instead of on the way I was feeling. It was much easier to deal with the physical pain than to deal with the storm of emotions that was going on inside my head. After that I hurt myself each time I was feeling bad. I had a hatpin that I used to jab into my leg and I used to buy cigarettes to burn myself with. I always covered up the bruises and the scars – I didn't want anyone to see what I was doing. No one ever knew about it. I just stopped when things started to sort themselves out in my life.'*

When someone hurts themselves like this, it's usually because there are things going on in their life that they feel desperately unhappy about and don't know how to control or change. Sometimes it's clear what has started these feelings – it could be that the person is being bullied or someone's treating them badly or they've got problems at home or at school – but sometimes the person isn't sure why they're feeling so bad. That can confuse and upset them even more.

If you're harming yourself, try to talk to someone about it. It doesn't have to be someone you know – you could talk to somebody on a helpline and you wouldn't have to tell them your name or where you were from. It's important to talk because when people self-harm they often feel very lonely and misunderstood. If you talk to someone, you'll feel less on your own.

Self-harming isn't a sign that someone's crazy – it's a sign that there's stuff going on in their life that they don't know how to deal with. A lot of people do it but it is dangerous. If you think that someone you know is hurting themselves then the best thing you can do is to talk to them and be their friend. They need support right now. But if you think they might be putting their life in danger, you need to get them help. If you think you can talk to them and decide together who to tell, that's great. If you can't, just try to let them know why you told someone who could help. Whatever they say, you'll have done the right thing.

# SUICIDE

It's devastating when someone commits suicide. When someone kills themselves, they're not only hurting themselves, they're also causing an enormous amount of pain to all the people who know them. If someone you know seems unhappy or withdrawn or is behaving in a weird way then talk to them. However they're feeling, they'll appreciate the fact that you've noticed they're not themselves, and if they are unhappy it will give them the chance to talk about it before it gets any worse. But if there's something that's making them unhappy and you think it's not going to be easy for them to deal with it on their own, encourage them to talk to an adult about it. They might not want to – and they might get narky with you for even suggesting it – but you need to do it. And if it's something very serious – like they're hurting themselves or someone's hurting them – then if they won't tell an adult you need to. If you do, they might accuse you of being a bad friend or betraying them, but the truth is you'll be being a good friend. In the long run you'll be helping them.

People are desperately unhappy when they start to think about suicide and they start to think that there's no way for life to get better. If this is how you're feeling then please take a couple of minutes to read this. Right now this might not seem possible, but situations *do* change and things *do* get better. Yes, this takes time and the stuff that's hurting you might not be easy for you to change on your own. But if you talk to people and let them know how you're feeling, you'll find they will want to help and support you. So often it feels like other people don't notice what we're going through, but if you talk to them you'll find they do care and they are there for you. You could try talking to your parents or your guardian or to a teacher or to your doctor or to someone on a helpline. Choose someone you trust.

You also need to look after yourself. Eat proper meals, do some exercise and make some time to do things you enjoy. That might be watching TV or listening to music or even just taking a bath. If it relaxes you, do it. Remember, the way you're feeling will change. Reach out, ask people to help you and give yourself time.

Remember, if you do commit suicide, the people left behind are the ones who suffer the most. As well as having to cope with all the grief of losing someone they love, they also often feel emotions like guilt and anger and rejection.

It is *not* your fault if someone you know commits suicide. You need to remember that. You also need to give yourself time to deal with what's happened and to go through the grieving and the unhappiness. It will help you if you can talk to other people about the way you're feeling and about your memories of the person who died. But when, with time, you start feeling happier again, don't feel down on yourself. It's good to pick yourself up and keep going with your life. It's the best way there is of remembering the person you cared about.

# 4 FAMILIES

*Stacy, 15, says: 'Mum and Dad divorced when I was eight. They're both remarried now and I've got a stepmum, a stepdad, two stepsisters and a half-brother. Sometimes I don't feel like I have a family – I just have a load of people getting in my face.'*

*Tamara, 14, says: 'I was put in foster care when I was three. Since then I've been with three different foster families. I keep hoping Mum will be able to have me back but so far it hasn't worked out.'*

*Richard, 15, says: 'I'm the only person in my group of friends whose parents are still together. I am grateful but sometimes I think they're the lucky ones – at least their parents never gang up on them!'*

Imagine this. You've just got together with the girl/boy of your dreams and you're taking her/him home to meet your family. Nervous? Heck, yeah!

That's the thing about families. Whether you're from a two parent, 2.4 children Simpsons set-up or your parents are separated/divorced/remarried/adoptive parents/foster parents/single parents/happy, hippy commune-dwelling parents – you can be guaranteed of one thing. At some stage, for some reason, you're going to wish they didn't live in the same place as you ...

Every family has disagreements. You can't put a bunch of people into one place and expect things to be fun the whole time. Problem is, it often gets less fun when you hit your teens. That's because you're growing up and want more space and privacy – and they're worried about letting you go. Freedom vs fretting = tension.

### So have you ever had this row?

→ **Your friends/ boyfriend/ girlfriend aren't good enough ...**
   When your parents don't like your friends it can feel like they're
   passing a judgment on you, especially when they don't even
   know them properly.

That's often the problem. Your parents don't know your friend and they might be getting the wrong impression. They're probably worrying because they love you and they don't want you to get mixed up with a crowd that would cause you trouble. If you want to solve this, you're going to have to explain to your parents what it is you like about this person and why they're your mate. If your parents have got the wrong idea about them, then talking to you should make them back off once you've convinced them they aren't a druggie/ rebel/ underground Mafia member. But if the reason you're hanging out with your friend is because they do drugs, bunk school or shoplift then, face it, you're not going to be able to convince your parents that this is someone you should be hanging around with.

→ **When you live under my roof you come in at a reasonable hour ...**
Your point of view: Curfews suck. Everyone else gets to stay out late. Why am I being treated like a child?
Your parents' point of view: We're still responsible for you. We're worried something will happen to you if you're out late. We're worried about what you're up to when you're out late.

So how do you come to a compromise? First off, remember that your parents think they're being strict for your benefit. They probably don't want to mess up your social life, they just want to make sure that as well as having a social life you're getting your work done and you're not out drinking, smoking, doing drugs and getting into trouble.

OK, but what about you? Why can't they give you some respect and let you make your own decisions about what's good for you? Well, if you want them to do that, you're going to have to prove to them that you deserve respect. That means talking to them (not yelling) about the way you feel and suggesting ways around the problem. Like ... how about they let you stay out later if you promise to get a taxi home and let them know exactly where you're going to be? Or ... how about you keep the curfew as it is during the week but make it later at the weekend? Or ... how about you have a trial run of a later curfew that stops if your social life starts messing up your work?

Hopefully, your parents will respect you for thinking about their point of view and for trying to do something constructive instead of having a strop – and hopefully that'll make them compromise too.

→ **You're not going out dressed like that.**
Parents can be so rude! Considering some of the stuff they wore when they were teenagers it's a bit much when they start to criticise your dress sense. But some parents just can't deal with a] their kids showing off what they've got or b] their kids being a bit alternative.

If your parents are the sort who are always banging on about your tops being too tight or your skirts being too short, then they're worried that people are going to notice you and harass you or even attack you. Unfortunately, they do have a point. There are people out there who think that certain clothes are an invitation to touch. It's compromise time again. If you're going out somewhere in public with a group of mates, then obviously you're going to be safer than if you're on your own or with only one or two other people. It's probably also safer during the day than it is in the evening or at night. But wherever and whenever you're going out it'll help your parents to relax if you wear shoes you can run in and if you take a coat to cover up.

If your parents are having problems dealing with your grunge/ rock/goth/whatever look, then they're probably freaking because this is a part of your life that they don't understand. If you can bear it, sit down and explain to them that you're not morphing into an alien, you're just into a certain type of music or culture and the clothes are a part of it. Once they see you're still you underneath, they should relax ... a bit.

→ **Why can't you be more like your sister/ brother/ neighbour's auntie's cousin's children?**
How annoying is it to be compared to someone else? Why do parents go shooting their mouths off and saying stuff like this without thinking? It's insensitive and it's not going to make you change. Plus if your brother or sister is sitting smugly anywhere near you it's just going to make you feel wound up with them too.

It's the sort of comment that makes you feel like your parents don't like you and wish you were someone else. Truth is they probably like you and love you but you've just got some habit that's driving them bonkers. It might be that your sister's really tidy but every time you leave the kitchen it looks like a Kansas whirlwind has passed through. It could be that your brother's a teacher's pet who never gets in trouble. It might be that your neighbour's auntie's cousin's children are never on the Internet right at the moment when your mum wants to make an important phone call. Whatever it is you're doing, it doesn't make you bad and them good – but if you want to make your parents shut up, the best thing to do is work out what you're doing that provokes them. Then you can try and make an effort not to do it. Hopefully, your parents will notice and you'll get some peace from the comparison police.

Hey, it's hard for parents when their kids hit puberty. It becomes really obvious that they're growing up and they don't need them the same way they used to. Plus, the hormone hotel that is any teenager's body is probably making them moody, emotional, angry, depressed and uncommunicative. That's not much fun for teenagers – but it's not much fun for parents either. It's not easy to talk to your folks about the way you're feeling but the more you let them in, the easier they'll find it to accept the changes going on in your life.

All that most parents want is to see their children happy and safe and making the most of their lives. They may well be annoying when they try to interfere but their excuse is a good one – they're doing it because they love you.

**Brother Bothers, Sister Shockers and Only Child Irritation**
There are loads of theories about how your position in the family affects your personality. Eldest children are meant to be more likely to want career success and they're said to be bossy, responsible and like to be in control. Middle kids are supposed to be a bit more laidback and diplomatic. The theory is they're a bit insecure and are more bothered about helping other people than focusing on themselves. If you're the baby of the family, you're meant to be the most likely candidate to become a party animal! Allegedly, youngest

kids are fun, outgoing and, well, a bit spoiled. Only kids are a right old mixture. They're used to getting their own way but they're also used to having their own space. They're meant to be high achievers with a stubborn streak.

It's probably true that your siblings – or lack of them – affect your personality, but this can be in all sorts of ways ...

*Tonya, 19, says:* '*My sister and I are twins. She's one of the most important people in the world to me and I love her to bits but it always used to get on my nerves the way everyone mixed us up. We're quite similar in our characters as well as to look at but we definitely make sure we emphasise our differences. She has her things and I have mine. For example she's very into looking after people and being a shoulder to cry on. I'm the more outgoing, party, social-life one. We decided we wouldn't even apply to the same universities so for the next three years we're both going to be in different cities. It'll be weird being without her but I'm looking forward to being known as me for a while!*'

*Ed, 18, says:* '*I've got a brother and a sister. I get on well with my brother but I can't stand my sister. She doesn't have a sense of humour and she's always telling my parents about stuff I've done. If I bring a girlfriend home and Liz likes her then I go off her!*'

*Felicity, 16, says:* '*My brother's autistic and that's definitely changed our family. I think it's made us much closer than we would have been otherwise. I've always felt responsible for him – and I've always felt bad that I'm able to go out and have a social life when he can't and my parents can't because they have to look after him. I always made sure I didn't get into any trouble because I didn't want my parents to have anything else to worry about.*'

*Alice, 15, says:* '*I always felt like my sister was better than me at everything. She was the pretty one and the brainy one and she's older than me so she'd done everything before me. But recently she told me that she used to think that way about me! Maybe we're both just paranoid ...*'

*Dan, 17, says:* '*I'm an only child. I don't know if it made a huge amount of difference because I always had mates who lived nearby that I could hang out with. I suppose I like my own company – but plenty of people who've got brothers or sisters do too.*'

There's a whole load of things that can cause fights between brothers and sisters ...

→ **Jealousy.**
→ **Telling tales.**
→ **When one keeps imitating the other or tagging along after them.**
→ **Not having enough privacy.**
→ **Having to share the phone, the Internet, the television, chores, etc.**

And then there are a lot of things that make it good to have them around too ...

→ **You've got someone to share the chores with.**
→ **You've got someone else to ask for advice.**
→ **You've got someone to hang out with on family holidays.**
→ **You've got someone to stick up for you.**
→ **You've got someone who understands what your family's like.**

The thing about families is that they're a lot of relationships going on in a small space. The bigger they are, the more complicated they get! Petty squabbles are something that everyone has to go through – but sometimes family life can get much, much more complicated ...

# SEPARATION AND DIVORCE

*Jenny, 15, says: 'I'd always been scared that my parents would separate because it had happened to most of my friends. I used to panic every time they argued. Then one night they had a row and Mum screamed at Dad that he should leave. He left and Mum just collapsed on the stairs, sobbing. Me and my sister were hugging her and crying too when Dad walked in and said he was sorry. It got sorted out and a few days later we all sat down and talked about what was going on. Dad and Mum had been having problems but they wanted to work them out. So far it's been OK and I feel a lot better now I know what's going on. Dad and Mum know that we don't want them to break up but they've kind of rammed the message home that even if they do it won't change the way they feel about us. I know that but it does help when they say it.'*

Why would two people who loved one another enough to get married or have children, get to a point where they have to split up? It's a scary thought – there's a part of everyone that wants to believe in the fairytale idea of happy ever after – but the truth is that people change. The person you loved in your twenties might not be the person who's right for you in your forties.

There are also things that can cause huge disagreements between people. Money problems or changing jobs or moving house can all cause a lot of tension. Often that tension is sorted out and your mum and dad will go back to normal – but sometimes the arguments can become so bitter that they end up driving people apart.

Every couple has things they find annoying about one another and everyone is guilty of doing things that irritate their partner. Staying together is a choice – but sometimes it can be better if people choose not to.

*Alex, 16, says: 'I knew my parents were going to break up. One or the other of them was in a bad mood all the time. After they divorced it took a few years for all the bad feeling to disappear but these days they're much more fun to be around.'*

*Col, 14, says: 'My parents ended up divorcing because my dad had an affair. Sometimes my mum acts like that made it all his fault but it wasn't. They'd been fighting for ages before he did that.'*

*Geoff, 15, says: 'I think my parents just got bored of each other. They weren't into the same things and they didn't even really have the same friends. They cared about one another but they weren't in love.'*

## So if they'd be happier apart, why is it so horrible when they split up?

It's tough breaking up with someone who's been important in your life. Even if both parents want the divorce, it feels sad that after so many years it's no longer right for them to be together.

That's made worse if one person wants to end the relationship and the other one doesn't. The one who doesn't isn't prepared for it to end and can end up feeling betrayed and angry and bitter. It can get nastier when your parents have to divide up their stuff. Sometimes major aggro breaks out over who gets the house or the car or the pets. If this is happening – let them sort it out for themselves. Half the time they'll say they're arguing over who gets what, but really that's just an excuse for having a go at one another about other things that have upset them.

It's awful for you because you feel stuck in the middle. It's a major change in your life and one that you can't do anything about. So you're stuck feeling sad and angry and scared and lonely and helpless. There are emotions flying around all over the place and it's bound to feel pretty rubbish ...

*Tony, 15, says: 'I know it's nobody's fault but I feel really angry. It's almost like I want to pick fights with people – just so I can let loose.'*

It's important for you to talk about the way you're feeling. If you bottle it all up, you can start to feel really isolated and depressed and like no one understands you. They will understand – but you have to let them in on what you're going through. If you're not sure what sort of response you'll get from your mates, try talking to someone older – or to someone from an organisation that's been set up to help people deal with this sort of trauma.

You've got a lot to deal with. You're trying to maintain your relationship with two people who are both really important to you but who aren't too hot on one another right now. Plus they might be leaning on you and wanting your support and that can drain your energy. Then you've got to come to terms with all the changes that separation and divorce bring with them – like moving home, like constantly swapping between two houses, like feeling different from your mates or responsible for your brothers and sisters. Sure, it's life – but it's not as you knew it. You're allowed to want some help from other people ...

It's good to talk about the way you're feeling and it's also helpful to get a bit of advice when it comes to the practical decisions you have to make – like which of your parents you're going to live with and when you're going to see the other one.

Usually, your parents will decide who it's better for you to live with and they might want to know if you've got a preference. Don't feel guilty if you do have a preference – it's your life and you're allowed to say what's best for you. After all, you might have a reason that isn't to do with preferring one of them, like your dad's moving away so if you went with him you'd have to change school, or you don't really get on with your mum's new partner. But if you don't want to have to say or you don't want to get involved, just tell them to sort it out between themselves.

If they can't sort it out between themselves, then they have to go to court and let a judge make the decision. That probably means a court welfare officer will come to your home to try and find out which parent you'd be better living with. They often – but not always – decide in favour of the mum.

Once the decision about who you live with has been made, a decision has to be made about how often you see your other parent.

Again, it's best if this is sorted out by your parents (with help from you) but unfortunately it doesn't always work out like that. Sometimes one of your parents doesn't want you to stay in contact with the other one – and sometimes you might feel like you don't want to see one of your parents.

## So what happens?

→ If one of your parents is trying to stop the other one from seeing you, then the one who's being prevented has to go to court and ask for a contact order. A contact order sorts out when they're allowed to visit, how long they're allowed to visit for and where the visit can take place. It might even have rules about who takes you to the meetings and who brings you back. If the court thinks one of your parents has got good reasons for not wanting you to see the other one, they can order all your meetings to be supervised. That means the court would send someone along to be at the meetings and to check everything's OK.

→ If you don't want to see your mum or your dad, then your other parent will have to go to court and persuade the judge that a contact order shouldn't be given. This isn't easy because the courts usually think that it's better for the children if they're in touch with both their parents. You might have to be visited by a court welfare officer and a child psychologist so the court can make sure you have good reasons for not wanting to see that parent.

Both your natural parents have a responsibility to make sure you're cared for and to help pay for the things you need. Usually, the parent who isn't living with you full time has to pay something called maintenance to the other parent. Maintenance is just a sum of money – the amount is decided by the court – that's contributed towards your living costs. If a parent doesn't pay, he or she gets chased for the money by the courts or by a group called the Child Support Agency (the CSA). But having a divorce can be tough on your parents' finances. Once all the dust has settled, you might find you can't do all the things you used to do – because suddenly instead of one house and car your parents are having to run two.

Plus they're both trying to develop new social lives. That means, yurk, your dad and your mum are going off on dates. First you have to watch them getting all gooey-eyed over someone who isn't your mum or dad – and then you might have to be prepared for yet more changes in your personal family tree.

It's easy to feel freaked out by the idea of your dad or mum getting together with someone else – and building a new family. Some people feel resentful because they feel like they're still dealing with all the fallout from the divorce while their parent is happily getting on with their life; some people feel upset because they know that their other parent isn't moving on so fast and will be upset to hear about the new relationship; some people don't like their parents' new partners and feel isolated in their own homes; and some people just don't want to have to cope with any more changes to their life.

*Kaz, 14, says: 'I didn't make any effort to get on with my dad's new girlfriends. For a start they were always changing and anyway, they all seemed really false. They made this big deal about wanting to impress me but they didn't really want to know who I was – they were just doing it to show Dad how nice they were.'*

*Duncan, 15, says: 'Mum hated the idea of Dad going out with someone new and I took that to heart a bit. When Dad met someone he really liked I almost sabotaged it. I didn't want to get to know her because I didn't think it was fair on Mum but then one day I overheard them talking and Dad's girlfriend was saying that maybe they should cool it because I obviously wasn't happy with the whole thing. When I heard how upset Dad was by that I realised I was being totally unfair to them. Mum and he were over and he should be allowed to be happy again. So after that I started making an effort and now I think Connie's really nice. She helps me get what I want out of Dad!'*

Your parents want you to be happy, so if you don't like their new girlfriend/ boyfriend they will probably think long and hard about staying with them. But if they're really loved-up, you might just have to take a big gulp and realise that this person is here to stay.

# STEP-FAMILIES

A step-family is the family you get when your mother or father marries again. So you can have a stepmum or a stepdad even when your real mum or dad is still alive. And if your stepmum or stepdad has children then you might find yourself with a whole load of stepbrothers and stepsisters.

Could be fun, could be not so fun. Whichever it is, step-families can take a heck of a lot of getting used to ...

*Madelaine, 13, says: 'My mum and dad divorced a long time ago but my mum has just married her long-term boyfriend and we've had to move into his house. It feels really strange. I've been here lots before but it's always been Giles' house and I feel like I'm a guest, not like I'm at home. It's even weirder on the weekends because sometimes his two daughters come to stay and we don't know one another very well. The youngest is my age but Kathy is two years older. She doesn't like Mum much and that makes me not like her so it's a bit awkward. Plus I've got her old room because it's the biggest and Giles said it's only fair that I should have it because I'm here all the time. I'm happy with that but I think Kathy thinks me and Mum are taking over.'*

*Anya, 16, says: 'I live with my dad and recently his girlfriend moved in. I like her but I'm not finding it easy having her here the whole time. I feel really disloyal to Mum – which is irrational – but it feels wrong to be saying "bye" to a different woman when I leave for school. Dad's worried because I'm spending a lot more time in my room than I used to but I can't talk to him about how I feel until I work it out for myself.'*

*Scott, 17, says: 'Dad and Mum got divorced last year because Dad had started seeing someone else. They've moved in together and I go to see them about once a month. I get on all right with her and she's got a son who's a year younger than me – Matt. It took a while but we're getting to be quite good mates. We're both into football and that helps because we sit in front of the TV and have a beer together.'*

First of all there's working out how to handle the idea of having an adult around who you've got to treat with respect but who isn't your parent. That's not easy – especially if they start acting like they are your parent and tell you what to do. You've got to work out a balance where you compromise, because you're all sharing a living space, but you don't feel like they're laying down the law and bossing you around.

If you can, it's a good idea to talk to your dad or mum and try to work out a way where you're all happy. It's important that you get:

→ **Time with your parent without their new girlfriend/boyfriend hanging around.**

→ **Privacy and respect from them. You're growing up and you've been through a lot. Sure, they're the adults but you have a right to express your opinions.**

→ **To treat the new stepmum/stepdad as a potential friend but that you're not forced into acting like they're a replacement**

**mum or dad. They're not. You'll work your own relationship out with them over time. No one should try and rush into playing happy families.**

It can take a long time – months, even years – to really sort out your own relationship with a step-parent. It is worth making the effort though, because they make your parent happy. Also, a step-parent can end up being a friend, an ally and someone you can go to for advice and friendship. You might not always want to do it but you should try to get along with them. Remember, it's probably just as awkward for them as it is for you!

But if you really make an effort with your step-parent and it's not working or you're unhappy, you need to talk to someone and try to sort things out. Maybe you could go and live with your other parent – or maybe you, your parent and your step-parent could go to counselling and try and work out what's going wrong. Having counselling isn't about being mad – it's just a chance to talk things through with someone who isn't involved. The counsellor will be able to stay neutral and point out to everyone what they're doing that's upsetting other people. It can really help.

Course, it might not be your step-parent who's getting you down. It might be your irritating little stepbrother or your snooty new stepsister.

Step-families get even more complicated when there are teenagers or children on both sides of the new family. Not only do you have to negotiate a new relationship with the adult who's appeared in your life – you also have to make an effort with their kids and watch your real parent doing the same. How many things could go wrong there? But, also – how many things could go right there? You might end up with a really good friend who you can hang out with whenever you want. You might end up with someone to talk to about your parents' divorce and how hard it was – after all, they've been through the same thing. And, even better, your new stepbrother/sister might have some really fit mates who keep dropping by ...

You didn't choose to have this relationship with your step-family and you might resent the time and space they all take up. But – reality-check time – they're here to stay. If you make an effort to think about how they're feeling and to try and get along, then it's all going to be a lot easier than it will be if you feel resentful and negative. You didn't create the situation – but you've got a big part to play in how the situation works out ...

*Niago, 14, says: 'Sometimes I wish it was just me and my mum at home. I get fed up when my stepbrother's being moody and won't say anything. But at other times it's nice having a brother to look out for me – and Mum's much happier with my stepdad than she was with my real dad. And it's always good at Christmas because I get more presents than I would have done otherwise!'*

## HALF-BROTHERS AND SISTERS

Of course, not every stepmum or dad comes complete with their own ready-to-go family. Sometimes they don't have kids but they decide they want them – with *your* mum or dad. That's a different scenario again. This baby's going to be related to you.

How would you feel if that happened? Pleased? Excited? Resentful? Or worried that as soon as the baby arrives you're not going to be of any importance at all any more?

*Pip, 16, says: 'When Dad told us he was having a new baby I was quite excited. By the time it arrives I'll be doing my A levels and then I'll be leaving home so it won't make much difference to my life and it might be really cute! But my sister Charlie's not happy with the idea. She's older than me so it makes even less difference to her life but she keeps saying she won't feel like the baby's sister and she doesn't want anything to do with it. She says she feels like that because she reckons Dad doesn't need the hassle of any more children – she thinks he should just be enjoying himself.'*

The way you feel about the idea of a new brother or sister depends on lots of things. It can be affected by:

→ How old you are.
→ How long it's been since your parents' break-up and how sorted you feel about that.

→ **How well you get on with your parent that's having the baby.**
→ **How well you get on with your step-parent.**
→ **How well your other parent has been coping since the break-up.**
→ **How big your house is.**
→ **Whether you'd have to live with the baby all the time or whether you'd just see it now and again.**

It stands to reason that there are some downsides to having a baby round the place. It's going to scream and cry sometimes, it's going to need lots of attention, it's going to cost a lot of money. It also means that your parent won't be able to do stuff with you as easily as they used to.

Some people worry that the arrival of a new baby will turn their step-parent into an evil witch (or wizard), who wants to get rid of them so that everything can be given to the baby and nothing has to be shared. OK, so they might not grow warts and a pointy nose, but when someone becomes a parent – especially for the first time – it's true that they might become a bit overprotective of the baby and a bit ratty with you. But that'll probably be because they're tired from looking after the baby and worried about how good they're being as a parent rather than because they've suddenly decided they hate you.

So those are things that can make a new baby seem like a terrible idea. But the good news is that there are also things that can make having a baby around really fun ...

→ **It's sweet .**

→ **It's a good source of money – hey, you're a built-in babysitter!**

→ **Your parents will start treating you more like an adult because they'll remember what a child really is.**

→ **It might bring you and your step-parent closer together.**

→ **Your real parent will want to make up to you for disrupting your life, so you might get closer to them.**

→ **When it starts to grow up it might become someone you're really close to.**

Once your mum or your stepmum is pregnant then the baby's on its way and you've got a choice to make. Do you get

narky about the new arrival and make yourself depressed –
or do you try and look at the good side? It's up to you – but at
the end of the day it's really a choice about how you're going
to make yourself feel ...

# ADOPTION

It may not even be that your parents or parent and step-
parent have their own kid. They might decide they want to
adopt a child. If they do want to adopt, they should talk to you
first and make sure it's something you'd be happy with,
because getting an adopted brother or sister is a bit
different to having a half-brother or sister, or step-siblings.

A child can be any age when it's adopted – from a baby up to
a teenager – and it might be very hard for them when they
arrive in your family, especially if they're older. After all,
something will have happened to them that meant they
needed to be adopted. Maybe their parents died, or couldn't
look after them properly, or hurt them. Whatever the
reason, it might take them a long time to feel safe in their
new surroundings.

### Who's allowed to adopt a child?
As long as you're at least 21 years old and you've never
committed certain crimes (especially violent crimes or
crimes against children) then you're allowed to *apply* to
adopt a child. It doesn't matter what age you are as long as
you're older than 21, it doesn't matter what sex you are and
it doesn't matter if you're gay or straight, single or married.

But a lot of people want to adopt and the authorities work
hard to make sure that children go to the right homes. They
want to know that the prospective parents are healthy, will
be able to care properly for the child and won't hurt them.

It's a big deal because once a child is adopted the adoptive
parents have got full legal rights for that child. That means
they've got all the responsibilities that a natural parent
would have for the child.

*Fran, 16, says: 'I'm adopted but as far as I'm concerned my adoptive parents are my mum and dad. They're the ones who've always looked after me and I love them. I know a bit about my birth parents but I'm not bothered about meeting them or anything.'*

## If you're adopted, do you get to keep in touch with your birth parents?

Yes! OK, it's not always suitable for you to keep in touch with your birth parents. If they abused or neglected you and that's the reason you've been adopted, then the authorities will probably decide it's not in your best interests to have contact with them. But if you've been adopted for other reasons, then these days the adoptive parents are advised to tell you all about your background and the fact that you were adopted. They're also encouraged to make arrangements for you to see your birth parents or keep in touch with them by letter – as long as the birth parents want you to. Sometimes it's too upsetting for them to have this contact with you and they find it easier to lose touch.

But it's your choice too. Make sure you talk to your adoptive parents and tell them how you feel about your situation.

## If I don't know who my birth parents are, is there any way to find them?

If you haven't been told about your birth parents before, then when you're eighteen you'll be given your birth certificate. That will have the names of your birth parents on it, along with the place you were born.

If your adoptive parents can't give you any information about them, then you could ask the adoption agency who handled your adoption for help. If that draws a blank, then you have to start doing some detective work. There are some useful contacts for this. The government looks after something called the Adoption Contact Register. You can register on that with your name and details – and if your birth parent also registers, they'll put you in touch with one another. There's also an organisation called Norcap (see 'Further Help' at the end of the book). They'll be able to give you advice and also talk to you about what to expect if you do track down your birth parents. It might be a great experience and you might even find that there's a whole new family who wants to welcome you in – but you might also find that you don't like your birth parents or that they can't handle you being a part of their lives. You'll also need to think about how your adoptive parents will feel when you set off to find your birth parents. They'll probably want what's best for you and hope that you find them and like them – but they might also feel a bit scared. They might be worried that you won't have time for them any more.

You've got to do what's right for you, but it'll probably help your adoptive parents if you reassure them that, even if you find your birth parents, it won't spoil the relationship you have with them.

## Fostering

Fostering is different to adoption because when you're adopted, the people you live with are the people who have legal responsibility for you. If you're put into foster care, the people who are legally responsible for you are your local authority (the council). Although your foster family are looking after you, you should have a social worker coming to see you regularly who can help you with any problems.

The other thing about foster care is that it's not necessarily permanent. You might get moved around from place to place or stay with one foster family for years.

*Marshall, 20, says: 'I always felt like other people thought it was my fault I was in foster care – it was because I'd been bad or something. But I was fostered because I was neglected as a baby. When social services found me and my sister in my mum's flat, we were both malnourished and I had anaemia. I got moved around a lot – and I don't feel that close to any of the people who fostered me. It makes you very self-reliant.'*

# WHEN THINGS GO WRONG

Whatever your situation is at home, things can go wrong. It can be really hard if someone you're related to has a serious illness or has a disability ...

*Harry, 13, says: 'My brother's autistic. He has to have special teachers and he finds it hard to make friends. I love him but I get annoyed with him sometimes – especially when I can't do things because my parents are busy looking after him and can't take me where I need to go. And some people bully him so I've ended up having fights with people about it.'*

Illnesses could be mental illnesses, physical illnesses, conditions like depression or anorexia or drug addiction. Whatever it is it can be a huge strain for the rest of the family and leave you feeling like your parents don't have time for you. You need to talk to them about how you're feeling, and it also helps if you get in touch with a support group in your area that looks after people who are in your situation. That will give you a chance to discuss how you're feeling with other people who know what you're going through.

Things can also go wrong at home when people who are meant to care about you treat you badly ...

*Erica, 25, says: 'I got put into foster care when I was ten months old because my real mum wasn't capable of caring for me. I personally did not have a good experience of fostering. My foster dad was an alcoholic and he was abusive. He used to scream insults at me. To begin with I didn't know my life was any different to other people's. I wasn't allowed to go and spend time at other people's houses and I wasn't allowed – and didn't want – people to come back to mine. I was ashamed of the things my foster father might say to them. And I was used to doing what I was told. My foster mother even decided what clothes I should wear – she would put my clothes out each day, knickers, socks, everything. I was really unhappy. I used to spend as much time as I could at school. I did netball, athletics, drama, anything that would keep me there for longer so I didn't have to go back home.*

*But it was impossible for me to say anything to anyone. I couldn't get the words out of my mouth to describe the way my foster father was. He was ill so everyone excused his behaviour anyway.*

*The one time I did try and tell my social worker what he was like she just dismissed it and told me I should make allowances.*

*Then when I was fifteen my foster mother told me she wanted to adopt me. That was the moment when I knew I had to do something. If she adopted me I'd be trapped in that family forever. I don't know how I got up the courage but I remember bunking off school, getting the bus to social services and telling them I needed to see a social worker. My social worker had left at that point and I didn't have another one assigned so I just said I needed to see anyone. In the end this young guy came out and I told him I was unhappy and I wanted to leave. I had to explain why but finally the guy said he'd get things moving.*

*I had to go to court and it took months before I was free. But I did get transferred to a different foster home and then when I was eighteen I was given my own flat. I hope things are different for other people but all I'd say to anyone who's unhappy is try to talk to someone you can trust. If you don't tell people what's going on, they can't help you. And if your social worker isn't helping then talk to someone like Childline and ask what you should do next.'*

Sadly, children do become the victims of abuse – physical, emotional and sexual. If that's all they've ever known, it can be hard for them to realise that what they're going through isn't normal or natural, but if you are unhappy or frightened or injured by someone in your family, you need to tell an adult you trust.

Never feel as though you're the one to blame and don't worry that you'll make things worse by telling someone. Abusers often tell the people they're damaging that they must keep quiet or they'll cause trouble. You won't. Talking about what's going on is the only way to make other people notice and help to get it stopped.

If you don't feel comfortable talking to a different person in your family, then why not try speaking to a teacher or a social worker or your doctor? If they all feel too close to home, then there are organisations like Childline or the NSPCC that have got people who are used to dealing with these situations and will know what you can do.

Another thing that you might have to cope with is the death of someone close to you.

*Will, 20, says: 'When I was fourteen my brother got leukaemia and died. He was a couple of years younger than me and I'd always been the one to look out for him. But one day when he was out on his bike he fell over and bruised himself really badly. The bruises didn't go away and Mum took him down to the hospital. That's when they found the leukaemia. He had chemotherapy and they thought there was a chance he'd be OK but he wasn't. When he died I didn't talk to anyone. I went to the funeral but I couldn't cry. I just couldn't really believe it was happening and that it was Ryan in that box. I refused to talk to anyone about it for ages – Mum and Dad tried to make me go to counselling but I didn't want to. I just acted like it hadn't happened and that I'd never had a brother, or I got really angry about little things and was really nasty to everyone. I don't know what got me out of it but slowly I began mentioning Ryan again – like on his birthday – and I suppose I just started to accept that he had died and it wasn't my fault and just because Mum and Dad missed him really badly didn't mean they wished it was me who had died. It took ages though and I still get upset when I think about it.'*

It doesn't matter how old you are, when someone close to you dies it's devastating. If they've been ill for a long time, then maybe you've had some chance to prepare for losing them but when their death is sudden your world gets shattered in an instant.

There aren't any answers or any quick ways to cope with what's happened; everyone finds their own way of getting through the unhappiness.

If someone's committed suicide, the feelings can be made even worse because people blame themselves, thinking that they might have done something or that they should have noticed how unhappy the other person was. It *wasn't* your fault.

It helps to talk. You're not imposing on other people by telling them how you're feeling – they want to be able to help. If you talk to your family and friends, they can help you and, importantly, you might be able to help and support them. If they knew the person who died, then they'll be hurting too. And don't feel like you can't show your feelings – you need to be able to grieve to come to terms with what's happened, and when you're ready you should let yourself start smiling and looking forward to things again. You can celebrate the person who died by living *your* life to the full.

## *RUNNING AWAY*

When things go wrong at home, sometimes people feel like their only solution is to run away. If you're feeling like you're reaching this point, then if there's anyone you trust enough to talk to – talk to them. If there isn't, then try ringing one of the helplines (like Childline) and talk to them about the way you're feeling. Running away might seem like an answer but in reality it's hard and dangerous and you could find yourself with bigger problems than you have at home. Remember too, that if you do run away, anyone who does care about you will be desperately worried about you.

But, sadly, people do run away – and some people feel safer on the streets than they do at home. If you are seriously thinking that you need to run away, then make sure you take some form of identification with you when you go. This means a passport, a driving licence or a birth certificate. With identification you'll find it a lot easier to get benefits than you will do if you can't prove who you are.

To find out which benefits you're eligible for you'll have to speak to someone at an advice centre or at a benefits agency. Look in the phone book to find the contact details of the ones in your area. You might get housing benefits or you might get some form of income support or jobseekers allowance. There are lots of rules governing who gets what and if you're under eighteen you might find it harder to make a claim. But it's still worth seeing what you can get.

If you've run away then you need to get in touch with one of the organisations that help homeless people. Don't sleep rough on the streets – contact them and find out where the hostels are that homeless people can stay in. They'll also be able to give you advice about getting a job and finding more permanent accommodation.

# 5 DRUGS

*Natasha, 15, says: 'I started smoking spliffs when I met my boyfriend Jason. He's three years older than me and him and all his mates were into it. I thought I'd look really young if I didn't join in. I only do it with them – I don't know where they get the stuff from so I couldn't get it for myself.'*

*Matt, 18, says: 'I take speed when I go out 'cos it gives me more energy and I find it easier to chat up girls when I'm on it. It makes me more confident. It's pretty rank the next day though – I just feel tired and really depressed.'*

*Jez, 16, says: 'All my mates are into drugs. There's not much else to do round where we live. I do it 'cos I like it and I don't see it's anybody else's business …'*

Let's face it, drugs are a fact of life. At some stage you or one of your mates are going to be offered something. Yeah, loads of drugs are illegal and you're not meant to take them – but at the end of the day the only person who can make those decisions about your lifestyle is you.

The important thing is that when you make those choices you know what you're doing and what's involved. So here's what you need to know …

## What is a drug?
A drug is a substance that can alter your mood. It's one word that covers a whole lot of different things. Alcohol's a drug, so is tobacco, so is heroin, so is aspirin. While your mum might not freak out if she saw you swallowing an aspirin, she's kind of likely to flip if she sees you with an E.

That's because although *any* drug can cause you damage if you misuse it, some drugs are considered to be a lot more dangerous than others. They're called 'controlled' drugs and there are tough laws against illegally possessing or dealing them …

Controlled drugs include:

**Amphetamines** (also known as amph, billy, black beauties, crank crystal, dexies, hearts, ice, speed, sulphate, uppers, whizz)

**Anabolic steroids** (also known as 'roids)

**Barbiturates** (also known as barbs, barbies, blue bullets, blue devils, gorillas, nembies, pink ladies, red devils, sleepers)

**Cannabis** (also known as bhang, black, blast, blow, blunts, Bob Hope, bush, dope, draw, ganja, grass, hash, hasish, hemp, herb, lights, marijuana, pot, puff, reefer, resin, sensi, sensemilla, shit, skunk, smoke, spliff, wacky backy, weed, zero)

**Cocaine** (also known as basuco, c, Charlie, coca paste, coke, dust, freebase, Gianlucca, gold dust, lady, Percy, toot, white base)

**Codeine**

**Crack cocaine** (also known as crack, gravel, rock, stone, wash)

**Ecstasy** (also known as Adam, brownies, burgers, disco biscuits, dolphins, doves, E, eckies, echoes, Edward, elephants, essence, fantasy, hug drug, love doves, M and M's, MDMA, MDMA powder, mitsis, Mitsubishis, New Yorkers, pills, rhubarb and custard, Rolexes, shamrocks, sweeties, tulips, white doves, X, XTC)

**Heroin** (also known as boy, brown, china white, dragon, gear, H, horse, jack, junk, skag, smack)

**LSD** (also known as acid, blotters, dots, microdots, tabs, trips)

**Magic Mushrooms** (also known as fly agaric, liberties, liberty cap, magics, mushies, 'shrooms)

**Methadone**

**Tranquillisers**     (also known as benzos, green eggs, jellies, jelly babies, mazzies, moggies, rugby balls, tems, tranx, yellow eggs)

*Katie, 13, says: 'A girl at school asked me if I wanted to come and have some poppers and I said yes 'cos I didn't know what they were. I thought they were sweets or something. And then when I saw the bottle and realised, I felt too stupid to say no. But breathing that stuff in made me feel headachey and sick. I wouldn't do it again.'*

# THE LAW ON CONTROLLED DRUGS

You're not meant to have these drugs. Full stop. If the police even think you might have them, they're allowed to search you then and there in the street – or to take you down to the police station to be searched.

If they're right and you do have illegal drugs on you, then you're in trouble. First off, they could tell your parents or your guardian. They might also give your name to Social Services and the Probation Service and you'd go down on their records. Then they'd make a decision either to give you a warning, or a formal caution, or to take you to court.

Even if it's the first time you've been caught, the police can still take you to court. They'd be charging you with possessing an illegal drug or with possessing with intent to supply.

If you're charged with possessing a drug, it means the police think you had the drug for your own personal use. If you're charged with supplying a drug, it means the police think you were going to pass the drug on to another person. It doesn't matter whether you were planning to share it, or give it away, or sell it – all of those things count as supplying.

If you're under eighteen, you'll be sent to a Youth Court for sentencing. Your parents might be fined or you might be sent to a Young Offenders' Institution. If you're eighteen or over, you could end up in prison.

The punishment you'd get would depend on how dangerous the drug is considered to be. In the eyes of the law there are three groups of drugs: Class A drugs, Class B drugs and Class C drugs. Class A drugs are considered to be the most dangerous.

## WHAT ARE THE CLASS A DRUGS?

Class A drugs include cannabis oil, cocaine, crack cocaine (crack is a form of cocaine that's shaped into small stones and smoked), ecstasy, heroin, LSD, methadone, processed magic mushrooms (ones that have been prepared for use), and any Class B drug if it's taken by injection.

If you're caught in possession of a Class A drug: the maximum sentence you'd receive would be seven years in prison and a fine.

If you're caught supplying a Class A drug: the maximum sentence you'd receive would be life imprisonment and a fine.

## WHAT ARE THE CLASS B DRUGS?

Class B drugs include amphetamines, barbiturates, cannabis and codeine. The government is considering changing cannabis from a Class B drug to a Class C drug but even if they do this, it will still remain a criminal offence to possess or supply it.

If you're caught in possession of a Class B drug: the maximum sentence you'd receive would be five years in prison and a fine.

If you're caught supplying a Class B drug: the maximum sentence you'd receive would be fourteen years in prison and a fine.

## WHAT ARE THE CLASS C DRUGS?

Class C drugs include anabolic steroids, mild amphetamines, minor tranquillisers and rohypnol.

If you're caught in possession of a Class C drug: the maximum sentence you'd receive would be two years in prison and a fine.

If you're caught supplying a Class C drug: the maximum sentence you'd receive would be five years in prison and a fine.

*Jo, 16, says: 'I get drugs for my mates when they want them. It started earlier this year – I kept noticing this really fit bloke around college. When I asked my mates about him they told me he was a dealer. So I thought buying some gear off him would make him notice me ...*

*I went up to him and asked him what he had. He said he had acid and I told him I'd take it. He told me I should just take half the tab at a time 'cos it was really strong stuff. I went home, sat on my bed and took half. After five minutes nothing had happened so I took the other half.*

*I thought he'd ripped me off 'cos I still wasn't having any reaction but then – after about twenty minutes – the whole world went crazy. I fell back on my bed and just lay there looking at the ceiling swirling around all over the place and making faces at me. My whole room's full of patterns – the curtains and the carpet and the walls – and everything was moving. First it would go really fast and then it all slowed down. I knew it was the acid but I started getting really panicky and thinking I'd taken an overdose. I went into the bathroom and stayed there for about an hour staring into the mirror and then I went back into my bedroom and wrote a letter to my parents telling them I was so sorry and I hadn't meant to kill myself – I was convinced I was dying.*

*I'd just finished it when Mum walked into the room and asked why I hadn't come through to see them. I was trying to be normal so I went with her into the sitting room and started watching TV.*

*They were watching a really lame programme – The Vicar of Dibley. I sat down with them and about two minutes later I was laughing so much I fell off the sofa. I kept saying, "I can't believe I didn't like this programme – this is the best programme I've ever seen".*

*Mum and Dad were giving me odd looks and I knew I was being really obvious so I went back into my room. I'd decided I wasn't dying so I ripped the letter up. But the whole night was weird. The LSD didn't wear off until about three o'clock in the morning and I kept crying 'cos I was convinced my parents knew I was on drugs and they'd hate me. Then I'd stop crying and just lie back on my bed and stare at all the stuff going on in my room.*

*And the next day in college was freaky. I felt really grey – like I didn't have any emotions. It was a relief when everything went back to normal. '*

# SO WHAT'S THE DEAL?

### Why are some drugs thought to be more dangerous than others?

Some drugs are more likely than others to make people addicted to them. These drugs make their users feel like they can't cope unless they're taking them. Some drugs cause physical dependency – if the user stops taking them they feel ill and shaky so they take more to make themselves feel normal again. Other drugs cause psychological dependency – the user has a craving to keep on and on taking them. Either way, the drug starts ruling their life.

So drug dependency is one danger – because if you're dependent on a drug you become an addict and feel like you need the drug to survive. But there are other problems with getting involved in the drug scene ...

One danger is that you never know what effect a drug is going to have on you. Even if it's a drug you've taken before, your body can still react badly to it. That might mean you feel sick or you scare yourself by having weird hallucinations and seeing things that aren't there – or, in the worst cases, people can end up dying. Don't think that just because your mates have tried it and they've been all right you'll be OK too. There's no way of knowing what that drug's going to do to you.

Another danger is that when you're given a drug, you don't really know what's in it. Some dealers – the people who sell the drugs – try and make a profit by adding cheaper ingredients into the drug. So they tell you they're selling you cocaine – and what you get given is cocaine mixed up with sugar. Do you really want to snort that up your nose? And it might not be just sugar that gets mixed in. It could be something really gross ...

You've also got to be careful that you don't take an overdose. Overdosing just means you take enough of the drug to cause yourself physical or mental problems. People die from taking overdoses. It can make their hearts fail – either because their hearts speed up too much or because their hearts stop. It can make their livers fail – which means dangerous toxins build up in the body – and it can stop people's lungs working so they can't breathe. If you think someone's overdosed, you need to get an ambulance as soon as possible and let the doctors know what you think the person's taken.

Then as well as all that there are dangers involved in getting the drug into your body …

Smoking drugs: This can lead to breathing diseases like asthma (difficulty breathing), bronchitis (coughing and difficulty breathing) or possibly even lung cancer.

Snorting drugs: Snorting a drug up the nose can damage the membranes inside the nose.

Inhaling drugs: Inhaling using a plastic bag can lead to suffocation.

Eating drugs: When people eat a drug the effect can come on very suddenly and make them very disorientated and likely to have accidents.

Injecting drugs: This is the most dangerous way of taking drugs. If people share their injecting equipment, they run the risk of contracting blood diseases like HIV or hepatitis (both of which can kill people) from the other users. The user doesn't know how much of the drug is going in and that means they're more likely to overdose. If they miss the vein when they inject, they can end up with abscesses (build-ups of pus) and gangrene (decaying tissue). They can also damage their body if they try and inject crushed tablets or capsules that aren't meant to be injected.

# WHAT THE DRUGS DO

## *AMPHETAMINES*

### The effects

Amphetamines are stimulant drugs – they speed up the body's reactions. Taking them makes people feel confident and energetic and really alert. But the comedown (coming down is what happens when the drug leaves your system) can go on for one or two days – or even longer – and make people feel depressed and tired.

### The downside

→ Amphetamines are sometimes injected and that causes its own problems ... (See 'Injecting drugs' on page 135)

→ Taking amphetamines can make some people feel tense and nervous.

→ If people take a lot in a short period of time, they can end up hallucinating (seeing and hearing things that aren't there) and get really panicked.

→ If people take amphetamines for a long time, they increase their risk of heart problems.

→ Using amphetamines a lot, for a long period of time, can cause mental illness.

### What does the law say?

Amphetamines are illegal. Usually, they're a Class B drug, but if they've been prepared for injection then they're considered a Class A drug.

### How do people take amphetamines?

They come either as tablets or as a grey/white powder. This can be snorted up the nose, swallowed, smoked, dissolved into a drink or injected.

## *ANABOLIC STEROIDS*

### The effects

People take anabolic steroids because they think the steroids will improve their muscles and let them exercise for longer. If they're used by people who exercise, they seem to build up muscle and make it easier for the body to recover from the exercise.

### The downside

→ One big problem is that anabolic steroids are usually injected and that causes a whole load of problems on its own, including risk of HIV and nerve damage. (See 'Injecting drugs' on page 135)

→ Boys who take anabolic steroids run the risk of suffering acne, growing breasts, having problems getting erections, their sperm count being reduced, their testicles shrinking, becoming sterile (unable to have kids), their liver failing and having a heart attack.

→ Girls who take anabolic steroids run the risk of suffering acne, their breasts shrinking, hair growing on their faces, their voices getting deeper, irregular periods and the possibility of suffering from miscarriage or stillbirth.

### What does the law say?

It isn't illegal to possess anabolic steroids but it is illegal to supply them. If you were caught with them and the police thought you were planning to pass them on to other people, you'd be done for having a Class C drug (see page 132).

Doctors can prescribe anabolic steroids – they're used to help people who suffer from anaemia (not having enough red blood cells) or whose muscles are weak after surgery. So the only legal way to get them is to have a prescription and get them from the chemist. Anabolic steroids are often associated with bodybuilders and sportspeople. But it's forbidden for professional sportspeople to take them as a way of improving their performance. If they're tested and found positive, they can be banned from ever competing again.

### How do people take anabolic steroids?

They either come as liquids to be injected or as a tablet to be swallowed.

## *CANNABIS*

### The effects

When people smoke or eat cannabis, it usually makes them feel really relaxed and everything seems more intense – especially things like music and colours. But coming down from the drug can make you feel tired. It also makes some people get the munchies – badly!

### The downside

→ Cannabis affects people's short-term memories, their co-ordination and their ability to concentrate. That means they're more likely to have accidents or do something dumb.

→ Cannabis can have a bad effect on people and make them paranoid and nervous.

→ If people smoke cannabis rolled up in a spliff or a joint and mixed with tobacco, it can lead to them getting addicted to cigarettes.

→ Health professionals think that people who smoke cannabis regularly for a long period of time may increase their chances of getting breathing problems and conditions like lung cancer.

→ A lot of people find cannabis addictive.

### What does the law say?

Cannabis is illegal to possess and to supply. At the moment, most forms of it (resin – a lump of cannabis or grass – leaves, stalks and seeds) are graded as Class B, but cannabis oil can be graded as Class A.

### How do people take cannabis?

People take cannabis either by cooking and eating it (be

careful if you get offered a hash brownie or something similar, because taking cannabis like this can make the effects much stronger) or by smoking it on its own in a specially designed pipe, or by rolling it up with tobacco inside a spliff.

## *COCAINE AND CRACK COCAINE*

### The effects

Cocaine gives people a 'buzz' and makes them feel really awake and confident and energetic. It's a stimulant drug, which means it speeds up the body's reactions. Usually, people take cocaine by snorting it up into their nose. The effects from one hit of cocaine usually last for about half an hour, but people who use it will often take more – because they get cravings for it or because they don't want to come down. Coming down from cocaine can make them feel tired and depressed. Crack cocaine is a type of cocaine that people smoke instead of snort. It has a more intense effect but it only lasts for about ten minutes so it's even more addictive than cocaine and the comedown can make people feel sick and restless.

### The downside

→ If people inject cocaine it can cause big problems. (See 'Injecting drugs' on page 135)

→ People have overdosed on cocaine and died.

→ Cocaine use can lead to heart problems and pains in your chest.

→ If people take a lot of cocaine they can have convulsions (where their bodies start spasming).

→ People snort cocaine up the inside of their nose and that can damage the nose. Ex-*EastEnders* star Daniella Westbrook ended up destroying her septum (the bit of tissue that divides the nostrils) by snorting too much cocaine and needed plastic surgery.

→ If people take too much cocaine too quickly, they can become paranoid and really confused.

→ Crack cocaine use can lead to heroin addiction because, after taking crack, people take heroin to help deal with the comedown.

→ A lot of people find cocaine really addictive.

## What does the law say?

Cocaine is illegal. It's a Class A drug so if you're caught in possession of it or supplying it, then you could face a severe punishment.

## How do people take cocaine and crack?

Crack comes in the form of small crystals that are smoked, and cocaine is a white powder that's either snorted or dissolved into a liquid and injected.

## *ECSTASY*

### The effects

Ecstasy is a stimulant drug. It speeds up the body's reactions and makes everything feel really intense. When people take it they get a burst of energy, which can last up to six hours, and feel really alert. But the comedown – feeling depressed and tired – can linger for days.

### The downside

→ There are concerns that using Ecstasy can lead to liver and kidney problems.

→ Ecstasy is often taken when people go clubbing. It can make people feel so energetic that they go on dancing for too long without taking breaks or drinking enough water. That can lead to overheating and dehydration.

→ Some health professionals are worried that taking Ecstasy can cause brain damage and depression.

→ People have died after taking Ecstasy.

**What does the law say?**

Ecstasy is illegal and a Class A drug. Other drugs, similar to Ecstasy, are also considered as Class A.

**How do people take ecstasy?**

Ecstasy is usually sold as a tablet. The tablets can be any colour, but the most common one is white. But be careful – Ecstasy's chemical name is MDMA and sometimes tablets are sold which claim to be MDMA but don't actually contain this chemical. The effects of those tablets on your body may be very different to that of Ecstasy. Ecstasy can also come in the form of crystals that can be licked off the finger or snorted up the nose.

*Tom, 19, says: 'The first time I took an E was at this illegal club in a warehouse in Bradford. It was me and my mate and our girlfriends. None of us had ever tried Ecstasy but we all wanted to so we each took one tablet. We were sitting cross-legged on the floor and then I started feeling really strange. It was like this huge rush going through my body – like a rollercoaster in my head. Both the girls puked up.*

*My whole body felt tingly and the beat of the music was actually inside me. It was great! I just wanted to get up and dance. But then my girlfriend collapsed. It was really scary. Her body was arching backwards and I could see all her muscles straining under her skin. Her eyes were wide open but I couldn't see her pupils.*

*Some bloke said she was having a seizure and I started getting really stressed. Everyone was coming up and discussing what we should do. They couldn't call an ambulance because it was an illegal club so they carried her through into this quiet bit. They wouldn't let me stay because I was E-ing my head off and getting in the way. They told me just to get out there and dance.*

*It was so surreal. I was really worried about her but everyone was trying to help her and I just fell in love with everyone for doing that. I'd just look at them and get this feeling of, "You're such a good person." I was out of it. Luckily my girlfriend came round in the end and decided she wanted to dance. She couldn't stand up – her body was sort of lolling around – so I held her under the arms and sort of swung her around. Everyone was buzzing because she was OK.*

*She felt terrible the next day though. We all did. I was really
miserable and tired and she kept getting hot and cold sweats.
Apparently the tablets we'd taken were pure MDMA ...'*

## HEROIN

### The effects
The first time people take heroin they often feel dizzy and a
bit sick, but, when they get used to it, it makes them feel
warm and safe. It can also make users feel relaxed and
sleepy, but if they take too much (an overdose) it can result
in them slipping into a coma or dying.

### The downside
→ Heroin is often injected, which is very dangerous (see
'Injecting drugs on page 135)

→ Heroin is very addictive, however it's taken. Once someone's
hooked it's very hard for him or her to stop taking the drug.

→ Heroin addiction is made worse by the fact that your body
starts to need more and more heroin to get the fix it's craving.
So people end up needing a lot of the drug just to stop
themselves from getting withdrawal symptoms and feeling
really ill.

### What does the law say?
Heroin is illegal. It's a Class A drug so if you get caught in
possession of it or supplying it, you could face a very tough
sentence.

### How do people take heroin?
Pure heroin comes as a white powder. When it's bought on
the street it's usually a brownish-white colour and not
completely pure. People either snort heroin up their nose,
smoke it or inject it.

## *LSD*

### The effects

LSD makes people hallucinate. They can see, hear, smell, touch or taste things that aren't really there. Reality becomes distorted and so does their sense of time and movement. The problem is that sometimes these hallucinations are good and sometimes they're bad and there's no way of predicting what they'll experience. It could be brilliant or it could be a nightmare – and it'll be different every time. LSD can last for as long as twelve hours and once someone's taken it they can't stop the effects.

### The downside

→ **A bad LSD experience can be hideous. People get terrified and don't know what's happening – sometimes they even forget that they've taken a drug and don't know what's causing them to feel like that.**

→ **If someone has a bad trip it can affect them for a long time afterwards and make them feel shaky and out of control.**

→ **While people are hallucinating they don't have control of their surroundings so it's easy for accidents to happen.**

→ **People who take LSD sometimes get flashbacks – re-experience their hallucinations – at random times after the drug has worn off.**

→ **Taking LSD can make conditions like depression or anxiety worse.**

### What does the law say?

LSD is illegal. It's a Class A drug.

### How do people take LSD?

LSD either comes as tiny tablets to be swallowed or as little quarter-inch-square pieces of paper. These squares of paper usually have a picture printed on one side but the picture doesn't mean anything. The pieces of paper are swallowed too.

## *MAGIC MUSHROOMS*

### The effects

Magic mushrooms make people hallucinate – see, hear, smell, touch or taste things that aren't really there. They have a similar effect to LSD but it's not as intense and it only lasts for about four hours. While people are on mushrooms they usually feel light-headed and really relaxed.

### The downside

→ Some types of magic mushrooms grow in the wild and people go and pick them. The problem is that they look very similar to some poisonous mushrooms that can cause serious illness.

→ Eating magic mushrooms can lead to stomach pain, diarrhoea and sickness.

→ Just like with any other hallucinogenic drug, users can have bad, upsetting and scary hallucinations.

→ Eating magic mushrooms can make mental conditions like depression or anxiety worse.

### What does the law say?

Magic mushrooms are classed as Class A drugs when they're prepared. It's OK to possess raw magic mushrooms, but if they've been dried, cooked or stewed, they're illegal.

### How do people take magic mushrooms?

People eat magic mushrooms raw, they eat them dried, they cook them in food or they stew them into a tea and drink them. If you eat a magic mushroom and start feeling sick, you should go straight to hospital and take a sample of the mushroom with you.

## *POPPERS*

### The effects

Poppers give people a head-rush and their faces and necks flush as their blood vessels enlarge. The feeling only lasts for about two to five minutes and afterwards people can get a headache.

## The downside

→ If people swallow poppers they can die.

→ Poppers make some people feel sick and faint.

→ If people use poppers regularly they can end up with skin problems around their nose and mouth.

→ If the liquid is spilled it can burn people's skin.

→ Taking poppers can cause serious problems for people who suffer from breathing or heart problems, from glaucoma (a disease of the eye) or anaemia (not having enough red blood cells).

## What does the law say?
Possessing poppers isn't illegal but it can be an offence to supply it.

## How do people take poppers?
Poppers is a liquid that is breathed in through the nose or the mouth. It comes in a small bottle or tube and is clear or slightly yellow-looking.

## *SOLVENTS (GASES, GLUES AND AEROSOLS)*

### The effects
Sniffing or breathing in solvents can make people hallucinate (see and hear things that aren't there). They can make people feel dizzy and light-headed. The effects last between 15 and 45 minutes but when it wears off it can cause headaches and make people feel sleepy.

### The downside

→ Even the first time someone sniffs gases, glues or aerosols it can kill them.

→ Solvent abuse (inhaling gases, glues or aerosols) can make people vomit, black out or suffer heart problems.

→ If people use solvents for a long time, they can end up with brain damage, liver damage and kidney damage.

→ When people use solvents they lose control of themselves and are more likely to have accidents.

→ Sometimes people inhale these substances by using a plastic bag over their head. This can cause suffocation.

→ If people squirt gases straight into their throats, they can flood their lungs with fluid and die.

## What does the law say?

Solvents aren't illegal, but it is illegal for a shopkeeper to sell gases, glues and aerosols to anyone under eighteen if they suspect they're going to inhale it. Shopkeepers are forbidden to sell gas-lighter refills to anyone under eighteen.

## How do people take solvents?

Solvents are inhaled into the lungs. Sometimes they're sniffed or breathed in off a sleeve or a cloth or from a plastic bag, and some gases and aerosols are sprayed straight into the throat.

## *TRANQUILLISERS*

### The effects

Tranquillisers slow down the body's reactions and make people calm (and a bit slow on the uptake). They stop people from feeling tense and anxious but they can also make them sleepy and forgetful. When people are trying to come off tranquillisers, they may experience panic attacks.

### The downside

→ If people crush the tablets or capsules and try to inject them, they can kill themselves. (See 'Injecting drugs' on page 135)

→ Tranquillisers can have a really dangerous effect if people drink alcohol while they're in their body.

→ Tranquillisers can be addictive. It's also possible for people to become tolerant to the effect of the tranquilliser and need to take more to achieve the desired effect.

## What does the law say?

It's not illegal to possess tranquillisers but it is illegal to supply them. If you're caught handing out tranquillisers, you'll be charged with supplying a Class C drug. There are also two sorts of tranquillisers that it is illegal to possess as well as supply. They're called temazepam (green eggs, jellies, jelly babies, mazzies, rugby balls, tems, yellow eggs) and flunitrazepam (Rohypnol). You're only allowed these if your doctor has prescribed them for you.

## How do people take tranquillisers?

Tranquillisers come in the form of tablets or capsules. Usually they're swallowed, but some people crush them and inject them.

# TAKE CARE OF YOURSELF

If you're going to take drugs, then there are things you can do to lessen the dangers involved.

→ Never share injecting equipment with anyone else – make sure you've got new, sterilised needles.

→ Don't try driving a car or riding a bike if you're on drugs – your reactions won't be in a good enough state and you're more likely to have an accident.

→ Be aware that drugs lower inhibitions. If you get high and then have unsafe sex, you're putting yourself at risk of infection or an unwanted pregnancy.

→ If you take a stimulant drug like Ecstasy, remember, you might feel like you have a lot of energy but you still need to take breaks and keep hydrated.

→ The mood you're in when you take a drug can have an effect on the way it makes you feel. So if you're feeling depressed or anxious, the drug might have a worse effect on you than if you are in a good mood when you take it.

→ If you've got a health problem, taking drugs could make that worse.

→ Try not to take drugs in dangerous places. If you're going to get out of it, then you don't want to be somewhere where it would be easy to have an accident or difficult to get help.

## So why do people take drugs?

Some people take drugs because it makes them feel good. Some people take drugs because it helps them deal with other things in their lives. Some people take drugs because of peer pressure. Some people take drugs because they started taking them and then they got addicted. Some people take them to get a reaction. Some people just take them because they're curious. And a whole lot of people take them without knowing what they're letting themselves in for ...

## Is it easy to tell if someone's on drugs?

No! It can be really hard to tell if someone's on drugs. Users can start to behave differently, their eating patterns and sleeping patterns can change and they can change friends – but those are all things that anyone can do, any time.

## What should you do if you reckon someone's addicted to drugs?

You know what it's like – if someone lectures you about doing something, it just makes you do it more. So there's no point in giving someone a hard time about taking drugs. At the end of the day, the only reason they're going to give up is because they decide to. But they might have been trying to give up – and they might be able to do it if they get a bit of support. The best thing you can do is talk to them, let them know you want to help if they want you to, give them the contact details of the groups that can help drug addicts (see 'Further Help' at the end of the book) and don't let them guilt-trip you into helping them hide what they're doing.

## What should you do if you're addicted to drugs?

If you're addicted to drugs and you want to clean up, then it'll really help you if you get in touch with one of the groups who help drug addicts (see 'Further Help' at the end of the book). They're people who know exactly what it's like because they've been there. You'll get information, practical help and, if you want to, you can meet other people who are going through the same thing. It's good anyway because it means you've got to get out instead of sitting in on your own feeling lonely and depressed and getting cravings for the drug. And make sure you look after yourself – coming off a drug takes time and you need to eat properly and get enough sleep.

## What should you do if someone who's taken a drug has a bad reaction to it?

| | |
|---|---|
| **If they've taken:** | Heroin, tranquillisers or solvents. |
| **They might:** | Get really sleepy. |
| **You need to:** | • Keep them calm. |
| | • *Don't* give them coffee to wake them up. |
| | • Put them in the recovery position (on their side, their upper arm under their head – not obstructing their mouth – and their upper knee bent). |
| | • If they keep acting oddly, call an ambulance and tell the crew what drug they've taken. |
| **If they've taken:** | Ecstasy, LSD, magic mushrooms or speed. |
| **They might:** | Panic and get tense. |
| **You need to:** | • Keep them calm. |
| | • Tell them they'll stop feeling like that soon. |
| | • Get them out of any crowds or bright lights or loud music. |
| | • If they start breathing too fast, get them to take long, slow breaths. |

**If they've taken:** Ecstasy or speed.

**They might:** Get dehydrated (not have enough water in their body). The warning signs that this is about to happen include getting cramps or headaches, fainting or getting really tired.

**You need to:**
- Take them somewhere quiet and cool (maybe outside).
- Try to cool them down.
- Make them sip non-alcoholic drinks like fruit juice (they need about a pint an hour).
- If they keep acting oddly, call an ambulance and tell the crew what drug they've taken.

**If they've taken:** Ecstasy, heroin, poppers, solvents or tranquillisers.

**They might:** Fall unconscious.

**You need to:**
- Call an ambulance and tell the crew what drug they've taken.
- Put them in the recovery position (on their side, their upper arm under their head – not obstructing their mouth – and their upper knee bent).
- Make sure they're breathing OK and that there's someone who can do mouth-to-mouth resuscitation if it's needed.
- Make sure they're warm but don't let them get too hot.

To learn how to do things like the recovery position and mouth-to-mouth resuscitation you need to learn some first aid. If you're interested in finding out about that, ring the Red Cross or the St John Ambulance. They'll be able to put you in touch with your local branch and you can go on a first-aid course.

Red Cross: 020 7235 5454
St John Ambulance: 020 7324 4000

# DRUGS DICTIONARY

**Abstinence:** Not using drugs.

**Acid:** LSD.

**Adam:** Ecstasy.

**Addiction:** A feeling that you cannot cope without taking the drug.

**Adulteration:** When drugs have got other substances mixed into them so that they're not pure.

**Alkyl nitrites:** A group of chemicals sold in liquid form. Give people a 'head-rush'.

**Amph:** Amphetamines.

**Amphetamines:** A stimulant drug that speeds up the body's reactions. Usually come in powder or tablet form.

**Anabolic steroids:** Drugs that increase muscle growth and stamina.

**Analgesics:** Drugs that act as painkillers.

**Anti-depressants:** Drugs prescribed for people suffering from depression.

**Barbies:** Barbiturates.

**Barbiturates:** Sedative drugs that slow down the body's reactions.

**Barbs:** Barbiturates.

**Basuco:** Cocaine.

**Bhang:** Cannabis.

**Billy:** Amphetamines.

**Black:** Cannabis.

**Black beauties:** Amphetamines.

**Blast:** Cannabis.

**Blotters:** LSD.

**Blow:** Cannabis.

**Blue bullets:** Barbiturates.

**Blue devils:** Barbiturates.

**Blunts:** Cannabis.

**Bob Hope:** Cannabis.

**Boy:** Heroin.

**Brown:** Heroin.

**Brownies:** Ecstasy.

**Burgers:** Ecstasy.

**Bush:** Cannabis.

**C:** Cocaine.

**Cannabis:** A drug with a mildly sedative effect that slows down the body's reactions.

**Charlie:** Cocaine.

**China white:** Heroin.

**Clean:** Not having drugs in your body.

**Coca paste:** Cocaine.

**Cocaine:** A stimulant drug that speeds up the body's reactions.

**Codeine:** A sedative drug that can be used as a painkiller.

**Coke:** Cocaine.

**Comedown:** The feeling you get as the effects of the drug wears off.

**Coming up:** The feeling people get when they take Ecstasy. It can make them sweaty, nauseous and feeling like their heart's speeding up.

**Crack:** Crack cocaine.

**Crack cocaine:** A form of cocaine that is sold in small lumps. It's a strong stimulant drug that speeds up the body's responses.

**Crank crystal:** Amphetamines.

**Craving:** A feeling that you've got to have something.

**Dealer:** Someone who sells or provides drugs.

**Dependence:** When you keep taking a drug because you want to keep a good feeling or stop a bad feeling.

**Depressants:** Drugs that slow down reactions and make people relax.

**Dexies:** Amphetamines.

**Disco biscuits:** Ecstasy.

**Dolphins:** Ecstasy.

**Dope:** Cannabis.

**Dots:** LSD.

**Doves:** Ecstasy.

**Dragon:** Heroin.

**Draw:** Cannabis.

**Drug testing:** When a physical checkup is done to see if someone has been taking drugs.

**Dust:** Cocaine.

**E:** Ecstasy.

**Echoes:** Ecstasy.

**Eckies:** Ecstasy.

**Ecstasy:** A stimulant drug that speeds up the body's reactions.

**Edward:** Ecstasy.

**Elephants:** Ecstasy.

**Essence:** Ecstasy.

**Experimentation:** Taking drugs to see what they do to you.

**Fantasy:** Ecstasy.

**Flashback:** Re-experiencing hallucinogenic visions sometime after first having them.

**Fly agaric:** Magic mushrooms.

**Freebase:** Cocaine.

**Ganja:** Cannabis.

**Gear:** Heroin.

**Getting stoned:** Feeling the effects of smoking or eating cannabis.

**GHB:** A sedative drug that relaxes the body.

**Gianlucca:** Cocaine.

**Gold dust:** Cocaine.

**Gorillas:** Barbiturates.

**Grass:** Cannabis.

**Gravel:** Crack cocaine.

**H:** Heroin.

**Hallucinogens:** Drugs that make people hallucinate – see or hear things that aren't there.

**Hard drugs:** Drugs that are thought to be dangerous and cause dependency (e.g. heroin)

**Hash:** Cannabis.

**Hashish:** Cannabis.

**Hearts:** Amphetamines.

**Hemp:** Cannabis.

**Herb:** Cannabis.

**Heroin:** A strong sedative drug that relaxes the body.

**Horse:** Heroin.

**Hug drug:** Ecstasy.

**Ice:** Amphetamines.

**Injecting:** Using a needle to insert a drug into your body.

**Jack:** Heroin.

**Joint:** Cannabis.

**Junk:** Heroin.

**Junkie:** A slang word for a drug addict.

**Ketamine:** A hallucinogenic drug that can cause people to see or hear things that aren't there.

**Lady:** Cocaine.

**Liberties:** Magic mushrooms.

**Liberty cap:** Magic mushrooms.

**Lights:** Cannabis.

**Love doves:** Ecstasy.

**LSD:** A hallucinogenic drug that can cause people to see or hear things that aren't there.

**M and M's:** Ecstasy.

**Magic mushrooms:** Mushrooms that can make people feel relaxed or have hallucinations (see and hear things that aren't there).

**Magics:** Magic mushrooms.

**Marijuana:** Cannabis.

**Mazzies:** Tranquillisers.

**MDMA:** Ecstasy.

**MDMA powder:** Ecstasy.

**Methadone:** A depressant drug that slows the body's reactions.

**Microdots:** LSD.

**Mitsies:** Ecstasy.

**Mitsubishis:** Ecstasy.

**Moggies:** Tranquillisers.

**Mushies:** Magic mushrooms.

**Narcotics:** Depressant drugs that relax the body.

**Nembies:** Barbiturates.

**New Yorkers:** Ecstasy.

**Overdose:** When you take so much of a drug your body can't cope.

**Percy:** Cocaine.

**Pills:** Ecstasy.

**Pink Ladies:** Barbiturates.

**Poppers:** Alkyl Nitrites.

**Possession:** Having a drug you're planning to take yourself.

**Pot:** Cannabis.

**Prescription only:** Drugs that have to be ordered by your doctor and bought at the chemist.

**Problem drug use:** When taking drugs starts to have a damaging effect on your life.

**Puff:** Cannabis.

**Recreational drugs:** Taking drugs for pleasure or to be sociable.

**Red devils:** Barbiturates.

**Reefer:** Cannabis.

**Resin:** Cannabis.

**Rhubarb and custard:** Ecstasy.

**Rock:** Crack cocaine.

**Rohypnol:** A tranquilliser that slows down people's reactions.

**'Roids:** Anabolic steroids.

**Rolexes:** Ecstasy.

**Sensemilla:** Cannabis.

**Sensi:** Cannabis.

**Shamrocks:** Ecstasy.

**Shit:** Cannabis.

**'Shrooms:** Magic mushrooms.

**Skag:** Heroin.

**Skunk:** Cannabis.

**Sleepers:** Barbiturates.

**Smack:** Heroin.

**Smoke:** Cannabis.

**Soft drugs:** Drugs that don't make the people who take them physically dependent on them.

**Solvents:** Gases, glues and aerosols that are inhaled and slow down the body's reactions. They can make the user feel drunk.

**Speed:** Amphetamines.

**Spliff:** Cannabis.

**Stimulants:** Drugs that speed up reactions and energise people.

**Stone:** Crack cocaine.

**Sulphate:** Amphetamines.

**Sweeties:** Ecstasy.

**Tabs:** LSD.

**Tolerance:** When the body gets used to a drug and stops reacting to it.

**Toot:** Cocaine.

**Tranquillisers:** Depressant drugs that slow down the body's reactions.

**Tranx:** Tranquillisers.

**Tripping:** Hallucinating – seeing or hearing things that aren't there – after taking a hallucinogenic drug.

**Trips:** LSD.

**Tulips:** Ecstasy.

**Uppers:** Amphetamines.

**Wacky backy:** Cannabis.

**Wash:** Crack cocaine.

**Weed:** Cannabis.

**White base:** Cocaine.

**White doves:** Ecstasy.

**Whizz:** Amphetamines.

**Withdrawal:** The shaky, ill feelings people have when they stop using drugs.

**X:** Ecstasy.

**XTC:** Ecstasy.

**Zero:** Cannabis.

# 6 ALCOHOL

How tasty does this sound? To make alcohol you just let fruit or vegetables or grains (oats and rye and barley and stuff) start to rot. As it rots bacteria begins crawling over it and so does a fungus called yeast. And this mixture of food and bacteria turns into ethanol – or ethyl alcohol. So when you have an alcoholic drink, what you're drinking is rotten fruit and bacteria, mixed up with flavoured water. Erm, yum!

The more ethyl alcohol (pure alcohol) is in a drink, the stronger the drink is going to be (and the more bacteria you'll be putting into your belly!). Take a look on the label for the letters ABV. That means alcohol by volume. So if a bottle says 37.5% ABV, it means that 37.5% of the contents of that bottle are pure alcohol. If you drank all that, you'd end up in a whole heap of trouble ...

*Chris, 18, says: 'I got wasted last week. This girl I fancied had asked me round to her flat. She likes tequila so I bought a bottle and she challenged me to a drinking game. We drank most of the bottle and then I got the spins really badly. I felt so rough. The room was going one way and I was going the other. She puked and that made me throw up. There were bits of sick stuck to her hair. Every time I look at her now I think of that.'*

You've got to remember that alcohol is a drug. Sure, it's a legal drug, but it's still a drug and that means it can mess you up. Alcohol's a depressant that slows down your body's reactions and makes you less in control of yourself ...

Alcohol can mess up your body by:

→ **Making you vomit (so your breath stinks, your throat hurts and your clothes are spattered in gunk).**

→ **Damaging your muscle fibres.**

→ **Giving you bloodshot eyes, a furry tongue and a blotchy face. (Sexy!)**

→ **Making you put on weight.**

→ Leaving you dehydrated. (When you're dehydrated you don't have enough water in your body.)

→ Giving you a hangover. (That's when you feel headachy, tired and shaky and a complete waste of space.)

→ Making you black out.

→ Slowing your reactions down and causing you to have an accident.

→ Slowing down your breathing and sending you into a coma.

→ Giving you cirrhosis (liver disease).

→ Giving you stomach ulcers.

→ Giving you heart and circulation disorders.

→ Causing brain damage.

→ Killing you.

It can also give you alcohol poisoning. Alcohol poisoning happens when someone drinks too much alcohol too fast and their body can't cope with it. People die from alcohol poisoning, so make sure you know what the symptoms are and what to do if it happens to one of your mates ...

The symptoms include:

→ Smelling strongly of alcohol.
→ Having cold clammy skin that can look pale or bluish.
→ Breathing really slowly.
→ Being semiconscious or unconscious.

If this happens to someone you need to:

→ Call an ambulance and tell the crew what's happened.

→ Put them in the recovery position (on their side, their upper arm under their head – not obstructing their mouth – and their upper knee bent).

→ Stay with them. People can still be sick when they're unconscious. If they're sick and the vomit stays in their mouth they might choke on it and die.

→ Keep them warm but make sure they don't get too hot.

Alcohol doesn't just damage your body. It can also make you do dumb things that get you into trouble. When people are drunk they're a lot more likely to put themselves at risk ...

→ **You might fall over – maybe even in the middle of a busy road.**

→ **You might argue with your mates for no real reason.**

→ **You might get it on with someone you don't fancy.**

→ **You might have sex without using contraception.**

→ **You might forget where you are.**

→ **You might get into fights.**

→ **You might hurt someone.**

→ **You might get into a car with someone else who's drunk and have an accident.**

→ **You might commit a crime.**

→ **You might deliberately hurt yourself because the alcohol's making you depressed.**

Plus when you're drunk you act in ways that make other people see you as:

→ **Untrustworthy (like when you start shooting your mouth off about the secret you promised your mate you'd never tell).**

→ **Aggressive (when you start picking fights or getting wound up over some stupid comment).**

→ **Easy (like when you declare to your crush how much you love them and then turn around and snog their best mate).**

→ **Stupid (like when you trip down the stairs and break your leg and your mum's favourite vase).**

→ **Dangerous (like when it suddenly seems like a really good idea to lie down in the middle of a busy road).**

You can never really tell what sort of effect alcohol is going to have on you. But if you are going to drink there are things you can do to stop it from being a bad experience:

→ **Don't drink when you're feeling down.**
Alcohol makes everything seem more intense. If you're out with

a bunch of mates having a laugh it'll probably make you hyper; if you're feeling chilled and relaxed it'll probably just make you fall asleep; but if you're feeling depressed it'll end up making you feel much, much worse.

→ **Don't drink too much.**
The more you drink the more likely you are to damage your body or even to overdose. Also, the drunker you are the more likely you are to do or say something you'll regret the next morning ...

→ **Don't mix alcohol with other drugs.**
This is really dangerous. Alcohol intensifies the way you're feeling and will exaggerate the effect of the other drugs on your body. Mixing alcohol and other drugs increases the risks of something bad happening – like you falling unconscious or overdosing.

→ **Be aware of your own limits.**
Different people can handle different amounts of alcohol without losing it. As a general guideline, the smaller you are the less you should drink because the effect of alcohol will hit you faster.

Basically, before you hit the booze, make sure you know exactly what you're messing about with. Everybody can handle a different amount of alcohol. It depends on their age, their size and their sex. Men and women's metabolisms (the chemical processes that happen in their body and change food and drink into energy or waste products) work differently. Men's metabolisms are usually better at dealing with alcohol, so it takes longer for their bodies to feel the effects of the drink. But that means they might be more likely to damage their body by drinking too much.

That's why the doctors have come up with a system to help people work out when they should stop drinking. Different types of alcohol are often different strengths, so it's not easy to compare one drink with another. Instead of saying you're allowed a certain number of drinks every week, the doctors say you're allowed a certain amount of alcohol units a week. One unit equals 10ml of pure alcohol or:

→ **250ml of average strength beer.**
→ **125ml glass of weak wine (9% ABV).**
→ **A 25ml (average pub measure) of spirits.**

Men aren't meant to drink more than 28 units of alcohol a week and they're not meant to drink more than three to four units a day. Women aren't meant to drink more than 21 units a week and they're not meant to have more than two to three units a day. Remember – this is the most alcohol adults are meant to have if they want to stay healthy, and they're also advised to have at least two days every week where they don't drink at all. And if you're a teenager, you should be drinking less than this anyway. Teenager's bodies are affected by alcohol much more quickly than older people's.

# THE LAW ON ALCOHOL

If a person is:

| | |
|---|---|
| Less than 5 years old: | It's illegal to give a child this age a drink. |
| 5 years and older: | Children aged 5 years and older can drink alcohol as long as they're not on licensed premises. (Licensed premises are anywhere you can buy alcohol – like a pub or a supermarket.) |
| 13 years and younger: | It's illegal for you to go into the bar of a pub, unless the pub has a 'children's certificate'. You are allowed to go into parts of the pub where alcohol is drunk but not sold (like the garden or a 'family room'). |
| 14–15 years old: | You can go into the bar of a pub but you're not allowed to drink alcohol. |
| 16 years and older: | If you're eating a meal in a pub you're allowed to have a beer or a cider with it, but you're not allowed to buy this at the bar. You have to be served in a dining area. |

Less than 18 years old: You're not allowed to buy alcohol. You're not allowed to buy it in pubs – or in licensed premises like off-licences or supermarkets. If you're under 18 and the police catch you drinking alcohol in the street, they're allowed to take it away from you.

18 years and older: You can buy alcohol in pubs and other venues but it's illegal for you to buy drinks for anyone under 18.

There are also laws about how much you can drink if you're going to drive. You're more likely to have an accident if you've been drinking. Legally, you're not allowed more than 80mg of alcohol for every 100mg of blood in your body. Everyone's different so some people will reach that level before others. The best thing to do is not to drive at all when you've been drinking.

*Sarah, 17, says: 'My older sister was killed by a drunk driver. She was on a zebra crossing at night and he just didn't notice her. He ran her over and didn't stop. Mum never talks about it but no one in my family would ever get in the car after they'd been drinking.'*

Alcohol can be dangerous. It can cause accidents and illnesses and, just like with any other drug, it can make you addicted to it. If you become an alcoholic – someone who's addicted to alcohol – then the troubles really start. Some people are psychologically dependent on alcohol. They feel they can't get through a situation unless they drink. They might feel like they can't get through a normal day without a drink – or that they can't get through parties without alcohol there to relax them. People can be psychologically dependent on alcohol even if they're not drinking that much. They start feeling very nervous if they can't get a drink or they might even have a panic attack.

*Ben, 19, says: 'When I was fifteen I found out that my dad wasn't my dad – he'd married my mum when I was little and adopted me. It really messed me up. I started having problems with him and then I started getting in trouble at school and I couldn't work out why I was feeling so bad. I felt self-destructive the whole time. I started drinking 'cos I wanted to hurt myself – I wanted to be out of it – and then it got to the point where I felt I couldn't cope unless I was drinking.'*

Other people are physically dependent on alcohol. They're usually people who regularly drink a lot. As people start to drink more, their bodies stop being affected by the alcohol as quickly as they used to. This means they've developed a tolerance for alcohol and they can drink more before they start feeling sick or out of control. The problem is that the amount they're drinking is damaging their body – badly. They're putting themselves at risk of life-threatening diseases like cirrhosis and at risk of having bad accidents. If someone's physically dependent on alcohol and they stop drinking for some reason (maybe because they're ill) they'll get alcohol withdrawal symptoms. They might be jumpy or have trouble sleeping or stop eating properly. They might get bad shakiness, have convulsions (fits), hallucinate (see things that aren't there) or even die. It's important for anyone who's giving up alcohol to talk to a doctor about how they should go about it so they do it safely.

Alcoholism causes all sorts of problems. Alcohol's expensive, so if you're addicted it can lead to a lot of money worries. Addiction can create problems at work or at school – stopping people doing their work properly or making them unreliable.

And alcohol can destroy families.

*Steve, 15, says: 'My dad's an alcoholic. Mum and he argue about his drinking and then he gets violent or storms out of the house and drinks more. I hate being around him and it makes me feel angry the whole time too.'*

*Lester, 18, says: 'The worst thing was always feeling helpless. I was always scared that Mum was going to hurt herself or someone else and there was nothing I could do about it. My parents split up and I used to go and visit her every weekend. I dreaded Sunday 'cos she'd drink all day and then she'd get in the car to drive me back to Dad's. I always sat in the front 'cos I felt more in control that way – I could tell her if she was in the wrong lane or if there were pedestrians up ahead. I couldn't wait to get out of the car but then I was terrified too – 'cos without me there I thought she was even more likely to have an accident. It was awful to love someone but not to be able to trust them – and to spend all your time scared of what they'd do.'*

*Lucy, 14, says: 'I can't tell anybody what it's like at home. I go round to my friends' but I never invite anybody back to mine – it's a dump. And I never know what mood Dad's going to be in when I get home. Sometimes he's acting crazy and sometimes he's just snoring in front of the TV ...*

*Emma, 17, says: 'Mum's been drinking since I was little. When I was younger I didn't know that she was an alcoholic – there were always bottles everywhere but she said they were apple juice and she never let us have any. And I didn't know that the way she behaved was different to the way other people's mums behaved. She was my mum and I loved her and I thought if she said something it was right.*

*She used to get angry if I showed any emotion. If I was upset or cried she'd scream at me and if I was happy and laughed I got screamed at too. I grew up thinking that it wasn't a good thing to show your emotions or let other people know anything about you. There was this one time when a girl at school was handing out invitations to her party and she said she'd done them all on different coloured paper. She said I should tell her my favourite colour and then I'd get the invitation on that colour card. That made me really angry with her because I thought she was trying to find out about me. I didn't want anyone to know me or get close to me because I thought if I let myself trust them they'd end up hurting me. So I didn't talk to anyone – not even my dad or my brother. Even when Dad left Mum and we all moved out I still couldn't talk about the way I felt. I loved Mum – I wanted her to be a part of my life – talking about her made me feel disloyal. I was terrified that she wouldn't be able to cope without us there or that she'd miss us so much she might hurt herself. But she didn't notice whether we were around or not. She's got wet brain – she's drunk so much that her mind isn't really able to absorb new information.*

*It hurt so much when I realised that. I was tearing myself to pieces about Mum and she didn't even know what she was doing. But luckily it was about that time that I started going to Alateen.*

*Alateen's a group for young people who've been affected by an alcoholic in their lives. We all sit round and talk about what's happened to us. Dad told me about it. I didn't want to go at first and it took me a while to start listening – but when I did it started to feel like a weight was lifting off my shoulders. It was because there were other people there who felt the same way as me and understood what I was feeling. It took months and months but I started making friends – I started realising that the only way I could get help was if I asked for it and that there would be some people who'd be willing to give it.*

*But I've got to reach out and try to be positive. I've got to remember that I'm me and I make my own choices about my life. I can't help my mum or save her. I can only help me.'*

If one of your parents is an alcoholic, it can affect you in all sorts of ways. It can make you feel responsible for them, it can make you feel ashamed and it can make you feel desperately unhappy. That can have an effect on your friendships, your schoolwork and your health.

But you're not to blame for your parents' choices. The best thing you can do is to get in touch with one of the groups (like Alateen) that have been set up to support people who've been affected by someone else's drinking. They'll understand what you're going through and they'll be able to offer you help and advice.

### How can you tell if someone's an alcoholic?

It's not always easy to tell. People who are psychologically dependent on alcohol might not actually drink very much and people who are physically dependent might be able to hide how much they're drinking. But there are some giveaways ...

→ An alcoholic may try to hide his/her drinking.
→ They might pretend to drink less than they do.
→ They might make excuses about why they drink.
→ They might avoid doing things where they can't drink.
→ They might deny that their drinking is a problem.
→ They might forget about things that happened when they were drunk.

→ They might always drink when they're upset or worried.
→ They might be arguing with their family, getting ill or not
turning up for things.

## Is there anything you can do to help an alcoholic?

It can take a long time for people to give up a drug like alcohol.
Even if they want to give up, the process can make them feel
ill and they can crave the alcohol really badly. It does help
them to have support, but remember that they have to want
the support – you can't force them into accepting it and you
can't force anyone to accept that they need help. It has to be
their decision and they have to want to do it.

The best thing you can do is talk to them, let them know you
want to help if they want you to, give them the contact
details of the groups that can help alcoholics (see 'Further
Help' at the end of the book) and don't help to hide or deny
what they're doing to themselves.

It'll probably also help if you go and get some advice and
support from one of the groups (like Alateen) that have been
set up to help people who've been affected by somebody
else's drinking.

## What should you do if you're an alcoholic?

If you're addicted to alcohol and you want to clean up, then
it'll really help you if you get in touch with one of the groups
who help alcoholics (see 'Further Help' at the end of the
book). You'll get information, practical help and, if you want
to, you can meet other people who are going through the
same thing. It's good anyway because it means you've got to
get out instead of sitting in on your own feeling lonely and
depressed and getting cravings for drink. It's also a good
idea to go and see your doctor. Withdrawing from alcohol
can be a difficult experience and your doctor will help you to
do it safely.

# 7 SMOKING

*Richard, 14, says: 'I hang out with a bunch of older lads and i reckon the fact I smoke makes them take me more seriously. It makes me look older too.'*

*Jessica, 15, says: 'I'd never date a boy who smoked. I think it's disgusting. It makes their mouths taste nasty and their teeth and fingers yellow. Why would anyone want to snog someone who looked like that?'*

So what do you think? Does smoking make you look older, sorted and in control? Or does it make you look a bit sad?

*Gina, 16, says: 'I used to be really anti-smoking when I was younger. I thought it stunk and it was dumb to spend all your money on something that would end up killing you. And I thought kids who smoked looked rough. But at college I got in with a bunch of different people and one day when one of my friends lit up I said, "Can I have one?" It was just an impulse thing – I suddenly decided I wanted to see what it was like. It tasted manky but I liked the feeling of having the cigarette in my hand. It's just gone on from there. I have about ten fags a day now ...'*

*Toby, 17, says: 'I started smoking when I was fifteen 'cos this girl I fancied wasn't interested in me. It was something to do to take my mind off it. But after a few months I realised I was getting more colds than I used to and it was getting in the way of my sports so I quit. I wasn't really addicted – and I'd got over the girl!'*

*Shannon, 16, says: 'When we went into the sixth form we got this common room and everyone smokes in there. It's just sociable.'*

People start smoking for a load of different reasons. Some get pressured into it by their friends, some people do it to piss off their teachers or parents, some people do it to look older or to lose weight or just because they feel miserable and want something else to focus on.

## But what exactly are they putting into their bodies when they smoke?

Cigarettes are made mainly of tobacco leaves. The leaves are dried, shredded and then either sold loose to be smoked in pipes or in roll-ups (cigarettes that people make themselves) or rolled up and sold as cigarettes. Tobacco leaves can also be in a powdered form – either as snuff (that is sniffed up the nose) or as snus (that is chewed or swallowed).

Tobacco contains nicotine – a fast-acting and addictive drug. The nicotine is the bit that gets people hooked on smoking. It's a stimulant drug. That means it speeds up the body's reactions but, unlike other stimulant drugs, it also seems to have the effect of making people feel relaxed. The problem is that as the effects of nicotine wear off, smokers start to get withdrawal symptoms and feel edgy and stressed. They don't realise they're feeling like that because of the nicotine, they think they're just stressed. So they smoke a cigarette to 'calm down' and the nicotine in the cigarette makes the withdrawal symptoms go away. But then they start to associate smoking with calming down and light up a fag whenever they get stressed.

*Anna, 18, says: 'I smoke to calm myself down. I started smoking when I was doing my GCSEs 'cos I was really worried about getting good grades. Now if something's getting me down I can easily get through a packet in a night.'*

When tobacco is burned it releases more than 4,000 chemicals that the smoker inhales. These include poisonous substances like arsenic (found in ant poison), phenol (found in toilet cleaner) and DDT (found in insecticide). Nice! But if it sounds manky to have those things going inside you, it's even worse to have two of the other things found in tobacco smoke ... carbon monoxide and tar.

Carbon monoxide is a poisonous gas. When it goes into your body it gets into your blood and reduces the amount of oxygen your blood can carry round to all your vital organs. That makes it harder for your body to grow, repair itself or to absorb the nutrients it needs. Carbon monoxide also affects people's hearts and can lead to fat being deposited on your arteries (the blood vessels that carry blood away from the heart). The fat can gather and start to block up the arteries and this can lead to heart disease and circulatory problems.

Tar is a thick dark liquid that gets inhaled and settles in smokers' lungs. As well as damaging the lungs, lots of the substances in tar are known to cause cancer in animals.

### What does smoking do to you?

Smoking can cause:

→ **Coughing**
→ **Sneezing**
→ **Shortness of breath**
→ **Wrinkles**
→ **Strokes**
→ **Gangrene (where body tissue decays)**
→ **Stomach ulcers**
→ **Heart disease**
→ **Lung disease**
→ **Osteoporosis (where bones get thinner and more likely to break)**
→ **Cancer**

It's not just smokers who are affected. When people breathe in smoke from other people's cigarettes, it's called passive smoking.

Passive smoking can cause:

→ **Uncomfortable eyes, noses and throats**
→ **Headaches**
→ **Sickness**
→ **Dizziness**
→ **Increased risk of asthma**
→ **Heart disease**
→ **Cancer**

*Lucy, 15, says: 'I know smoking can make you ill but I keep on smoking 'cos I'm worried that if I don't I'll put on weight. At the moment if I get hungry I have a cigarette and the hunger goes away. I know it would be healthier to exercise but I hate running ...'*

## Why do people find it hard to quit smoking?

→ **Nicotine's addictive.**
   If people stop smoking, they get withdrawal symptoms and start feeling stressed and unwell. It's the effect of their body craving a drug fix.

→ **Smoking can make people feel like they're part of a group.**
   If their mates smoke then it becomes a ritual they do together.

→ **People can feel insecure and nervous without a cigarette.**
   It's a prop for them to hold on to.

→ **Smoking's a habit.**
   People are used to smoking at a particular time, like after they've eaten, or in a particular situation, such as when they're stressed or bored. It takes a lot of willpower to change a habit.

*Dan, 17, says: 'I'm quite shy. When I'm out with my mates – down at the pub or whatever – I find it easier to relax if I've got a cigarette. It gives me something to do with my hands and if I haven't got anything to say I can smoke instead.'*

## What happens if people do quit?

→ **They get withdrawal symptoms. These can include depression, disturbed sleep, hunger, edginess and a lack of concentration. These symptoms will probably last around a month.**

→ **Cigarettes cost a lot so they'll save money.**

→ **Their breathing will improve and they'll be able to do more exercise without feeling tired.**

→ **Their clothes, hair, skin and breath will stop smelling of smoke.**

→ **They'll stop getting so many coughs and colds.**

→ They'll be able to taste and smell things more easily.

→ Their lungs will start to heal.

→ Their risk of catching a smoking-related disease will start to go down.

# 8 MONEY

One of the most annoying things about being a teenager is not having enough money to do all the things you want to do. For some people, it's even worse than that and they find themselves in a situation where they don't even have enough money for food. No one in this country should have to be in this position. The social services departments in every council should be providing enough money for everyone to have basic food and shelter. If you or your parents are really struggling for money then you must make sure you're getting all the benefits you're eligible for. It might be that you're allowed something like free school meals but you haven't been getting them. Get your parents to talk to social services and check what you're entitled to.

Hopefully you're not in this position and your parents are able to give you a bit of cash or help you out when you want new clothes. But this might still leave you annoyed that you can't go to that match or buy that CD. In that case, your best bet is to get a part-time job. But until you're fourteen you haven't got a heck of a lot of options when it comes to getting a job. That's because until then you're not *meant* to work. OK, so most people do a spot of babysitting or do a newspaper round before then, but don't even bother asking for a shop job until you're well and truly an official teenager.

Even then there are a load of laws that govern what you're allowed to do until you're sixteen ...

→ You're not allowed to work during school hours.
→ You're not allowed to work before 7 a.m. or after 7 p.m.
→ You're not allowed to work for more than two hours on any school day.
→ You're not allowed to work for more than two hours on a Sunday.
→ You're not allowed to work anywhere where there's a risk of you being injured.

Once you are sixteen you're allowed to work full time if you've left school, but you're still not allowed to work in a bar or in a betting shop until you're eighteen. If you're staying on to do A levels or retake your GCSEs then you're not going to have time to do a full-time job, but you do get one bonus! You're now eligible for an NUS student card. They cost £6 but they're well worth shelling out for because you can use them to get loads of discounts. If you're at college you'll be offered one automatically, but if you're staying at school then you can get an NUS Associate card. This costs exactly the same as an NUS card and gets you all the same benefits. All you have to do is ring the NUS Associate card hotline on 0870 241 4128 and ask for an application form.

Getting special discounts is one way of saving money when you buy things, but you also need to be sussed about saving money to spend later. Once you're fourteen you should be able to get yourself a bank account and a cash card to go with it. Don't get carried away by the special offers that some banks do – like a £20 music voucher. What you should be checking out is the amount of interest you'll be paid on any money you pay into your account. If you're not too old it might be a really good idea to get a children's savings account because these often offer very good rates of interest. And look at building societies and online bank accounts too – you might find you get a better deal with them than with the banks. Building societies quite often don't offer cheque books, but then you probably won't be able to get a cheque book from a bank until you're putting money into your account regularly (i.e. you have some sort of income). You almost definitely won't be able to get your hands on a credit card until you're over eighteen. But even when you can bag a credit card – be careful. With a credit card you can buy stuff even if you don't have the money in the bank – you just have to pay it back within a certain timescale. But some people go mad as soon as they get a credit card and start buying things they really can't afford and running up big debts.

*Jude, 19, says: 'I loved having a credit card. I booked a flight and took my boyfriend away on holiday to Italy and I bought a load of new clothes. When the bill came in I couldn't afford to pay it and so the bank added interest to the amount I owed. It just seems to keep going up and up and up.'*

If you're feeling really loaded, the other thing you could think about is putting some money into an ISA. ISA stands for Individual Savings Account and it makes more money than money in a normal account because you don't have to pay tax on it. You can't open an ISA until you're sixteen and you might not feel like you have enough money coming in to worry about saving it – heck, you're too busy out spending it! But stuff is expensive and there may well be things in your future that you want to save for – like university or your first car. Even if you don't have enough money to save right now, it's still a good idea to get your head round financial issues – so that when the money does start rolling in you'll know what to do with it! That's why it's a good idea to get involved in a group called Young Enterprise. This is a company that helps people aged from 14–19 set up a business for a year. You get taught how to come up with a business plan, get investors, run it and liquidate it! It's a really good way to get your head round balancing budgets and keeping a steady cash flow – and, even better, you get to keep any profits you make during the year it's in existence. Your school might be in touch with Young Enterprise but if it's not, check them out on the web and give them a call.

The Young Enterprise experience also offers you the big benefit of having something really useful to put on your CV. Face it, before long you're going to be applying for jobs and you need to show those future employers that you're worth however many thousands of pounds they're going to pay you every year to work for them. So how do you do that? First off, you need to get as many good grades as you can. But that's not all you want on your CV. Employers want to know that you're capable of holding down a job (and not everyone finds it easy to get up at seven o'clock in the morning and get into work on time). They want to know that you'll fit in with the rest of their employees and that you'll be a nice person to work with. So how do you convince them of that? Easy – get as much work experience as you can and make sure you're also involved in things outside your school work that interest you. Erm, sadly that doesn't mean hanging out with your mates – it means being on a sports team or raising money for charity or doing things that will impress people with your skills.

You might not know what you want to do with the rest of your life right now – that doesn't matter – but the more stuff you find out about, the more options you'll have. So get out there and make the most of all your opportunities – and good luck!

# FURTHER HELP

NUMBERS BEGINNING 080 OR 0500 ARE FREEPHONE. IT WON'T COST YOU ANYTHING TO PHONE THEM AND THEY WON'T SHOW UP ON YOUR PHONE BILL.

## ORGANISATIONS THAT CAN HELP YOU WHATEVER YOUR PROBLEM

Childline: 0800 1111
Childline is the UK's free, 24-hour helpline for children and young people with any problem.

Children's Legal Centre: 01206 873 820 (Open Monday–Friday 2–5 p.m.) You can get free legal advice and information about any issue.

Get Connected: 0800 096 0096
Whatever problem you've got you can ring Get Connected and discuss it with them. They'll be able to tell you which helpline will be the most useful and they'll even put you through to them so you won't have to pay for the phone call. You can call Get Connected any day between 4 p.m. and 11 p.m.

NSPCC (National Society for Prevention of Cruelty to Children): 0808 800 5000 (Textphone users – deaf or hard of hearing – 0800 056 0566)
The NSPCC takes calls from anybody concerned about their own or another young person's safety.

The Samaritans: 08457 90 90 90
A 24-hour helpline for anyone with any problem.

www.childline.org.uk
The Childline website.

www.nspcc.org.uk
This is the NSPCC's website. Contains information and advice for young people.

www.getconnected.org.uk
>    Website where you can find services to help you,
>    whatever your problem.

## FURTHER CONTACTS FOR PEOPLE CONCERNED ABOUT PHYSICAL HEALTH ISSUES:

Eating Disorders Association Youth Helpline: 0845 634 7650

This helpline provides people you can talk to about worries over your eating or someone else's eating. It's open from 4–6.30 p.m. on weekdays and outside these hours there's an answerphone so you can leave your number and they'll ring you back (you can also e-mail the Eating Disorders Association on info@edauk.com).

NHS Direct: 0845 46 47
>    This helpline is open 24 hours a day and offers free
>    medical advice and information.

Toxic Shock Syndrome Information Service: 020 7617 8040
>    Information about toxic shock syndrome.

Acne Support Group: 020 8841 4747
>    This group offers support and advice to people suffering
>    from acne.

www.edauk.com
>    Information about eating disorders.

www.nhsdirect.nhs.uk
>    This is the NHS Direct website.

www.stopspots.org
>    This is the Acne Support Group website.

www.tssis.com
>    This is the Toxic Shock Syndrome Information Service
>    website.

www.wiredforhealth.gov.uk
>    A website containing lots of health information.

# FURTHER CONTACTS FOR PEOPLE CONCERNED ABOUT SEXUAL ISSUES:

The Beaumont Society: 01582 412 220
　　A self-help group for cross-dressers and their families.

British Agency for Adoption and Fostering: 020 7593 2000
　　Advice and information on adoption and fostering.

British Pregnancy Advisory Service: 0345 30 40 30
　　Advice and information about abortion and the morning-after pill.

Family Planning Association: 0845 310 1334
　　Offers advice and information on contraception and all aspects of sexual health. They'll be able to give you the contact details of your local family planning and sexual health clinics.

The Gender Trust: 07000 790 347 (until 10 p.m.)
　　A national self-help group for people concerned about gender issues.

London Rape Crisis Centre: 020 7837 1600
　　Advice for anyone, anywhere in the UK, who has been raped or sexually abused.

Mermaids: 07020 935 066 (until 9 p.m.)
　　A self-help group for under-19s who are confused about their gender identity and their families.

Youth Access: 020 8772 9900
　　Advice, information and counselling in your area.

Brook Advisory Service: 0800 0185 023
　　For contraceptive and sexual-health advice and to find out your nearest young person's clinic.

Lesbian and Gay Switchboard: 020 7837 7324
　　If you've got questions about your sexuality or you want contact details for lesbian and gay groups in your area, then these are the people to try. The switchboard is open 24 hours a day.

Marie Stopes Information Line: 0845 300 80 90
　　For information on abortion.

National Aids Helpline: 0800 567 123
    Confidential help and advice 24 hours a day.

National Council for One Parent Families: 0800 018 5026
    Advice and help for single parents.

NHS Direct: 0845 46 47
    24-hour advice line.

Sexwise: 0800 282 930
    Advice about sex and relationships for the under-19s.

Survivors UK: 020 7357 6677 (Tues 7 p.m. – 10 p.m.)
    Advice and support for young men who've been raped or
    abused.

The Terence Higgins Trust Helpline: 020 7242 1010
    Information, help and advice on HIV and AIDS.

www.lovelife.hea.org.uk
    Information on STIs, HIV, AIDS and sexual health.

www.ruthinking.co.uk
    Information on sex, contraception, abortion and STIs.

www.baaf.org.uk
    Information on fostering and adoption.

www.likeitis.org.uk
    The Marie Stopes International Youth website. Has
    information on all aspects of sexual health.

www.survivorsuk.org.uk
    A website for young men who have been raped or
    abused.

www.mermaids.freeuk.com
    Information about gender issues for the under-19s.


## FURTHER CONTACTS FOR PEOPLE FACING EMOTIONAL DIFFICULTIES:

Anti-Bullying Campaign: 020 7378 1446 (or e-mail
    help@bullying.co.uk)
    If you're being bullied, you can ring up and get support
    and advice.

Kidscape: 020 7730 3300
A charity committed to keeping children safe from harm and abuse.

Cruse Bereavement Care: 0870 167 1677
Offers advice and counselling to anyone who's been affected by a death.

Eating Disorders Association Youth Helpline: 0845 634 7650
This helpline provides people you can talk to about worries over your eating or someone else's eating. It's open from 4–6.30 p.m. on weekdays and outside these hours there's an answerphone so you can leave your number and they'll ring you back (you can also e-mail the Eating Disorders Association on info@edauk.com).

www.edauk.com
Information about eating disorders.

www.bullying.co.uk
Advice for people who are being bullied.

www.mindout.net
Information about mental health issues.

## FURTHER CONTACTS FOR PEOPLE FACING FAMILY PROBLEMS:

Alateen: 020 7403 0888
Confidential help and advice for young people whose lives have been affected by somebody else's drinking.

British Agency for Adoption and Fostering: 020 7593 2000
Information and advice for anyone involved in adoption or fostering.

Carers National: 0808 808 7777 (Monday–Friday 10 a.m. – 12 noon, 2–4 p.m.)
Can give you details of your local Young Carers project. Young Carers are people who look after relatives or friends.

Relate: 01788 573 241 / 0845 456 1310
Relate is an organisation covering England, Wales and

Northern Ireland. It offers advice and support to people suffering from relationship problems.Relate also have a counselling service for teenagers called Relateen. If you contact Relate they'll be able to tell you if there's a Relateen service in your area.

Sane: 08457 678 000 (2 p.m. – 12 midnight)
Can give information, support and details of local services to anyone with a mental illness – or their friends and families.

Write Away: 020 8964 4225
Provides pen pals for young people with brothers or sisters who have disabilities.

Youth Access: 020 8772 9900
Provides information on your nearest free advice, information and counselling services.

Centrepoint: 020 7426 5300
This is a charity that helps homeless people aged 16–25.

Crisis: 0870 011 3335
This is a general enquiries line for Crisis, a charity working for the homeless.

Cruse Bereavement Care: 08457 585 565 (Monday–Sunday 3–9 p.m.)
A counselling service for anyone who's suffered from the death of a friend or a relative.

Eating Disorders Association Youth Helpline: 0845 634 7650
This helpline provides people you can talk to about worries over your eating or someone else's eating. It's open from 4–6.30 p.m. on weekdays and outside these hours there's an answerphone so you can leave your number and they'll ring you back (you can also e-mail the Eating Disorders Association on info@edauk.com).

The Line:  0800 88 44 44 (Monday–Friday 3.30–9.30 p.m.; Saturday–Sunday 2–8 p.m.)
This is Childline's service for young people who live away from home or who are in care.

National Association for the Children of Alcoholics: 0800 289 061

This is a helpline for people who are affected by their parents' drinking.

National Drugs Helpline: 0800 776 600
Help and advice to anyone worried about their own or somebody's else drug use.

Shelter: 020 7505 4699
You can ring Shelter to find out who to ask in your area for information on housing rights.

Survivors UK: 020 7357 6677 (Tuesdays 7–10 p.m.)
A helpline for young men who've suffered sexual abuse or rape.

Who Cares? Trust: 0500 564 570 (Monday, Wednesday and Thursday 3.30–6 p.m.)
Information and help for young people in residential or foster care.

www.thewhocarestrust.org.uk
Information for people in residential or foster care.

www.gurney.org.uk/eda
Information for anyone worried about eating disorders.

www.youngminds.org.uk
Information about mental health and mental health problems.

www.survivorsuk.org.uk
Advice for boys who've been the victim of sexual abuse or rape.

www.al-anon.org/alateen.html
Information for young people whose lives have been affected by somebody else's drinking.

## FURTHER CONTACTS FOR PEOPLE CONCERNED ABOUT DRUGS:

Adfam National Helpline: 020 7928 8900
This is a helpline for anyone who's worried about one of their friends or family being involved in drugs. It's open Monday, Wednesday, Thursday and Friday from 10 a.m.

to 5 p.m. They'll ring you back so you don't have to worry
that the call will cost too much or that it'll show up on
your phone bill.

National Drugs Helpline: 0800 77 66 00
The National Drugs Helpline offers free and confidential
advice about drugs. You can get information,
counselling, find out about people who can help in your
area or just have a chat – 24 hours a day.

Release: 020 7729 9904
This is a confidential helpline where you can find out
about drugs and the laws on drugs. It's open 24 hours a
day.

Families Anonymous: 020 7498 4680 (Monday–Friday 1–4
p.m.)
If you're worried because one of your friends or family is
involved in drugs then Families Anonymous can put you
in touch with people in your area who are going through
the same thing.

Narcotics Anonymous: 020 7251 4007
Narcotics Anonymous is a network of self-help groups
for drug users. If you're involved with drugs and want
help, they can put you in touch with a help group in your
area.

www.ndh.org.uk
This is the National Drugs Helpline website where you
can get advice and information about drugs.

www.cascade.u-net.com
This is a website where you can get information about
drugs.

# FURTHER CONTACTS FOR PEOPLE CONCERNED ABOUT ALCOHOL:

Drinkline: 0800 917 8282

> You can call Drinkline if you're worried about your own drinking or about the drinking of someone else you care about and you'll get confidential help and advice.

National Association for the Children of Alcoholics: 0800 358 3456

> This helpline is open from 9 a.m. to 7 p.m. Monday–Friday, and there's a 24-hour answerphone so if you ring outside those hours they'll call you back. It's for advice, someone to talk to or for useful contacts in your area.

Al-Anon/Alateen: 020 7403 0888

> Al-Anon and Alateen are groups that offer understanding and support for people who are affected by someone else's drinking. Al-Anon is the adult group and Alateen is for young people aged between twelve and twenty. If you ring the number, they'll be able to give you details of your local group.

Alcoholics Anonymous: 020 7833 0022

> Alcoholics Anonymous offers support and information to individuals who have a problem with drinking.

Families Anonymous: 020 7498 4680 (Monday–Friday 1–4 p.m.)

> If you're worried because one of your friends or family is involved in drugs, then Families Anonymous can put you in touch with people in your area who are going through the same thing.

www.hexnet.co.uk/alanon

> This is the Al-Anon and Alateen website.

## FURTHER CONTACTS FOR PEOPLE CONCERNED ABOUT SMOKING:

Quitline: 0800 00 22 00 (9 a.m. – 9 p.m.)
> Quitline offers help, information and advice to smokers. It's open seven days a week.

NHS Smokers Helpline: 0800 169 0169
> This helpline offers practical advice and information to smokers as well as practical tips on how to give up.

www.ash.org.uk
> This website has got loads of information on smoking as well as tips on how to give up.

www.quit.org.uk
> Lots of advice on how to give up smoking.

## FURTHER CONTACTS FOR PEOPLE CONCERNED ABOUT MONEY:

www.nusonline.co.uk
Advice for students.

www.princes-trust.org.uk
The Prince's Trust helps people improve their skills and get training. If you're facing any problems with getting a job, this is a good place to look for help.

www.young-enterprise.org.uk
Information on how to start a young enterprise scheme.

www.cpag.org.uk
The Child Poverty Action Group's website. Information for children living in poverty.

# INDEX

# ACKNOWLEDGEMENTS

Thanks to all the organisations who sent information (many of whom are listed in the back of this book) and special thanks to all the people who shared their experiences. Your names have been changed but you know who you are!

Also, thanks to Bina Abel from The Market Place, and, at Virgin Books, Ray Mudie, who had the original idea for this book, and my editor, Mark Wallace, who made it happen.